# SMILE,
# IT'S ONLY
# TELEVISION

# SMILE, IT'S ONLY TELEVISION

## THE ADVENTURES OF A TV REPORTER

## Nigel Farrell

*CARTOONS BY DON OSMOND*

BLANDFORD PRESS
POOLE · DORSET

First published in the U.K. 1984
by Blandford Press, Link House,
West Street, Poole, Dorset, BH15 1LL

Distributed in the United States by
Sterling Publishing Co., Inc.,
2 Park Avenue, New York, N.Y. 10016

**British Library Cataloguing in Publication Data**

Farrell, Nigel
  Smile, you're on television.
  1. Farrell, Nigel  2. Television broadcasting
  of news—Great Britain—Biography
  I. Title
  070.1'9'0924          PN1992.4.F/

ISBN 0-7137-1404-2

Typeset by Graphicraft Typesetters Ltd.
Printed in U.K. by
Biddles Ltd., Guildford

# ACKNOWLEDGEMENTS

The author would like to thank the following for their help: Marian Hatt, Keith Bloodworth, Ian Whiteley, Steve Panton, Ron Longman, Mike Smith, Jenni Murray, Bruce Parker, Enid Hewitt, Pippa Copp for unscrambling the M3 recordings, Don Osmond for his superb cartoons, and Mo Farrell for encouragement, great help and invaluable advice on taste — only some of which was heeded.

To the men who built the M3 motorway
upon which most of this book was written

# 1

The Prince of Wales stopped suddenly in his tracks and gave me a very chilly stare indeed.

His abrupt decision to cease forward movement took the small group of aides, detectives and grinning civic dignatories walking a few paces behind completely by surprise and they toppled into one another like dominoes. The crowd fell into a hush; from just behind me I could hear the gentle purr of the film camera in the sudden silence.

Prince Charles' eyes drilled into me like a pair of long steel screws.

At last he spoke.

'Why did *your* parents call *you* Nigel?', he asked icily.

Now there are some moments in the life of a television reporter which are stickier than others, and this was one of the stickiest so far. Prince Charles was on an official visit to a hospital in Portsmouth, an occasion which coincided with the long-awaited announcement that the Prince's newly-born baby son had been given the Christian name of William. Ever since the famous birth of the Royal Infant a few weeks before, there had been endless speculation over names for the second-in-line to the throne; would it be James, or Philip or Henry? Today was a 'quiet' news day and the announcement that William was the surprise final choice became the unrivalled major story of the day in bulletins on radio and television. It was not, however, the easiest story to cover; the Prince and Princess of Wales had made it quite clear that they would not be giving interviews on the subject and short of publishing the barest details Buckingham Palace was maintaining a lofty silence.

I had set off earlier that morning to cover what I assumed to be yet another routine Royal visit for local television. Just as I was arriving at the hospital the car's VHF radio that connected me directly to my newsroom in Southampton bubbled into life.

'Base calling Nige, base calling Nige!'

This was the husky, cigarette-worn voice of Don, my producer,

and it filled me with dread. Don allocated the reporters'
assignments, and over the years he had given me some pretty
painful jobs. His voice was quite excited now, and that was worse
than ever.

'Nige, it's Willy, it's Willy!'

'Pardon?'

'It's Prince William, that's what the little nipper's going to be
called, it's just been announced. London say will you stick a
microphone up Charlie's nose and ask him why he's chosen the
name Willy ... the whole world wants to hear, so don't cock-up
this one, got it?'

Now I've covered many visits by members of the Royal Family in
my time and I won't be playing things down if I tell you I have
grown to hate them. They're a newsman's nightmare; planned
months in advance, the route, actions, footsteps, handshakes and
smiles are mapped out and timed to the last second. They are utterly
predictable occasions, not helped by the fact that reporters,
photographers and film crews are allocated specific areas from which
they must not stray. Unscheduled attempts to 'doorstep' interviews
with Royal personages en route are regarded as offensive and are
strictly forbidden, particularly when it has been made clear that
certain questions are taboo, i.e., 'Why have you chosen the name
Willy, Charlie?' A step out of line meant 'trouble with the Palace'
which resulted in the withdrawing of facilities for future events and
the blacklisting of the offending reporter. On this occasion the very
large lady in charge of the press corps accompanying the Royal
party had particularly reminded us all to behave. 'There has been a
recent inclination for camera crews to try getting microphones to
within earshot of the Royals, and this must stop,' she announced.
She was wearing a flat straw hat that looked as though someone had
sat on it, and a very tight-fitting black cotton dress which revealed
rippling muscles and shoulders the size of a well-exercised ox. We all
nodded agreement.

It was with a certain feeling of trepidation, therefore, that I
strategically positioned myself, along with Mike the cameraman and
Tim the soundman, beside the main entrance to the hospital out-
patients department at which I knew His Royal Highness would
emerge at any moment. It was very hot and the recent natal

activities in the Royal Family had brought out a huge, happy crowd. Every time one of the doors opened and an official popped his head out into the sunshine to check no one was standing in the way the crowds surged excitedly forward, cheering and waving their plastic Union Jacks like medieval peasants bribed to put on a good show. They made me nervous; I had an uncomfortable feeling that when the Royal party finally appeared they would charge like a herd of stampeding elephants and neither Mike, Tim nor I would ever be heard of again.

Then there was Prince Charles, surrounded by his entourage of immaculate cronies, and as he moved off at high speed I realised that if I didn't act quickly the moment would be lost for ever.

'Sir, sir!' I shouted rather louder than I had planned. Heads turned imperiously. 'Sir, how is the Royal Prince today? Is he well?'

I thought this would be an innocuous opening gambit with which to hook the Prince and, although he kept walking, His Royal Highness did indeed turn to observe this insolent subject. Noticing the camera and still enjoying the novelty of being a father, he couldn't resist saying: 'Fine, thank you, fine,' but his expression quickly returned to stone. An imposing man in glittering uniform beside him looked at me sternly, his face reading like a Royal Protocol Instruction Manual: you should not have asked, but you have, and you have got away with it. Now go and boil your head.

The procession picked up speed again.

'Sir, sir!' I shouted again, feeling rather like a small insect about to be stamped upon. 'Why have you decided to call him William?'

This was altogether more serious. More heads turned, asking themselves who on earth was this persistent little man and his silly questions? Hadn't he been told to keep off the subject? Hadn't the Palace said no interviews?

The Prince had already flashed around again, although he was walking faster.

'What is *your* name?' he asked.

This threw me completely. For a moment my mind went a total blank, and the best I could do was to trot along beside him muttering like an imbecile.

Then suddenly I remembered.

'Nigel, sir.'

9

It was at this point that Prince Charles came to his unexpected stop, so that the whole Royal Party had to throw on the emergency brakes and everyone just avoided falling flat on their faces. The aides and officials began eyeing me like vengeful hawks; this was not on the schedule.

The insect was about to be swotted.

'Why did *your* parents call *you* Nigel?'

Now I don't mind admitting that this was not at all what I had intended. After all, I was supposed to be extracting an interview from *him*, not the other way around.

'Er . . . um . . . er . . .'

Like a drowning man, I seized a cork-like distant memory that I suddenly spotted bobbing past.

'I think it was because my father was very friendly with a fellow fighter-pilot in the RAF during the war called Nigel and it was a name they liked,' I said rapidly without drawing breath, adding quickly, 'Sir.'

Upon hearing this the Prince's face suddenly relaxed and with a shimmer his anger had gone. This was a world he understood and respected.

'The RAF?'

'The RAF, yes sir, yes sir indeed. Oh, yes sir.'

'How very interesting.' I had broken through. 'Well, oddly enough, it was rather the same in *our* case. William was a name we liked and as well as that, it wasn't a name which had been used in the Family for some time.'

He was warming to the theme now, and it slowly dawned on me as he was speaking that I was securing a world scoop. With the easy familiarity of an old friend I was just about to pop another question when I became aware of the fact that I was in motion.

At first I couldn't quite put my finger on it. Then I realised that my body was being propelled backwards at high speed. It had nothing whatsoever to do with my legs; I was simply in reverse, as if I was being sucked out of the way by a gigantic Hoover.

Straining to look over my shoulder, I gradually realised what was happening. The Amazon in charge of the press party had seized the back of my jacket and was simply hauling me away. I had entered

10

*'Why did your parents call you Nigel?'*

the 'total exclusion zone' and had to be removed. Just like that.

It was a curious sensation. There was nothing I could do, of course, save wave rather pathetically at the Prince as I was dragged away. He looked completely bemused.

I was towed around the corner of the block and given a verbal beating-up. I was actually quite annoyed at having been so rudely interrupted, but she was bigger than me so I kept mum until the working-over was complete. After a list of dire threats I was finally released. I noticed with satisfaction that she had somehow lost her ghastly straw hat in the fracas.

Don was overjoyed. In the circumstances my short, rather undistinguished interview was indeed an exclusive and was broadcast around the world, although in the unlikely event of my meeting Prince Charles again I shall probably be given a wide berth.

I mention this encounter because some days later it struck me that being quizzed by the Prince of Wales about the origins of one's Christian name in the course of one's normal duties was a rather bizarre way to earn a living. Then, reporting for television is an odd activity; and when I came to stop cursing it for a moment and consider it seriously, I decided that it was this bizarre element which made it such fun, and to hold down a job which is fun is a privilege.

It's a job which has given me a passport into the lives of other people; it has been a licence to meet Prime Minister and gipsy, film star and surgeon — butcher, baker and candlestick maker. I have interviewed Chief Constables and murderers, Bishops and pro-stitutes, Olympic athletes and dying men. I've had breakfast at the Ritz, a picnic lunch at Broadmoor top security prison and dinner with the captain of the QE2. I have driven a chieftan tank, been hugged by a boa constrictor and interviewed a man who could play 'Land of Hope and Glory' by bashing his skull with a bent spanner. The salary's a bonus.

Like most television journalists my career was fostered in newspapers. As a tadpole I worked as a trainee reporter on a traditional weekly paper in Sussex, where I drove my shorthand teacher into early retirement, and dreamed of discovering so stunning a story that I would never have to work again. Growing bigger and more confident, I hopped across to a daily evening newspaper and, after a year growing fat and lazy and chasing fire-engines only when they drove right past my front door I managed the jump into local radio. Here journalism took on a new dimension: it was fast, furious and very exciting, with few stones under which to hide. After a few years of racing around the South of England with a long line of magnetic tape trailing behind me I was lean and hungry enough for the leap into television, and the fact that I made it into a fully-developed television toad is due in large part to great good fortune.

My broadcasting career began with the BBC and upon publication of this book will probably end with the BBC. At this point let me make my position unequivocal: I believe the British Broadcasting Corporation to be the finest broadcasting organisation in the world. No doubt about it. Oh yes, really superb. In the unlikely event of my present boss reading this let me add that he particularly has made an outstanding contribution to world broadcasting.

Nevertheless, it must be said that over the years the BBC has developed some curious practices and one of the most prominent of these is the BBC Board.

Every applicant for a permanent job in the BBC must go before a BBC Board. This consists of no less than five people who sit along one side of a long table, like the guns of a battleship; isolated on the other side of the table sits the applicant. One by one the Board members take pot-shots at this unfortunate person and if at any stage he fails to answer a question in the correct manner he will receive a broadside. It is designed to be as gruelling as possible and it is. Unfortunately, what it frequently tends to test is not one's skills as a broadcaster but one's ability to withstand a five-man verbal barrage from a range of only a few feet.

One humble hack summoned to a Board a few years ago has now become a legend within the BBC Appointments Department and those who are worried at the prospect of their own Board, as I was, are reminded of his performance in the hope they will draw some consolation from it.

This was a man short of temper for whom the odious BBC Board was nothing more than irritating waste of time. As the interrogation proceeded he became more and more angry. He fought to control his fury, for he knew that his future lay in the hands of his five masters but at last, his face puce with rage, he could bear their questions no longer. Retaining as much dignity as he could possibly muster, he slowly stood, thanked the Board, and walked out of the room.

At least, he *thought* he walked out of the room. In fact he strode coolly over to what transpired to be the door, not of the room, but of a small cupboard. It was only when he had opened it and was already stepping forward that he realised his mistake. For a moment he gazed blankly at the contents of the cupboard, an old, balding mop with what looked like a piece of dried seaweed hanging from it, and a rusty bucket.

The panel of inquisitors watched, fascinated, as their candidate, looking neither to the left nor the right, completed the step inside the cupboard and closed the door softly behind him.

Patiently the Board members waited for him to reappear, but after several minutes of embarrassed silence one of them tiptoed over to

13

*The candidate ends his interview with the BBC Board.*

the cupboard, opened the door to reveal the poor man cowering in the shadows praying no one had noticed his mistake and led him, shame-faced, across the room and to the safety of the corridor outside.

He didn't get the job.

My application to become a BBC television reporter involved a double ordeal; not only had I to face the awful Board, during which I was to receive a real roasting which reminded me of the days spent in the Headmaster's study trying desperately to stuff handfuls of blotting paper into my underpants — a ploy, for those innocents amongst you, to remove the sting from beatings — but for the first time in my life I had to do an audition. This was a terrifying prospect, and had I known that all the candidates' auditions were relayed to every television set in every office on the station so that all the staff could have a good laugh I would never have applied in the first place.

Armed with a new suit, a haircut, clean nails and a desperate desire to camouflage a boil that was developing on the side of my nose, I found my own way to the studio through the busy corridors of the old converted hotel that was now the BBC's main broadcasting headquarters for Southern England. It had once been a grand palace for millionaires stopping over for the night before embarking for America on the big transatlantic liners which used to sail from Southampton with such frequency; now it was a fast-fading monument to a former, grander age, and amongst its pillars and richly-decorated, massive ceilings the trappings of television and radio appeared curiously incongruous.

Right in the heart of the building was the single studio, windowless, soundproof, air-conditioned, black, the ultimate in artificially-controlled environment. It was a weird sensation, walking into it, rather like stepping into an anonymous black box suspended somewhere in space. There seemed no contact with the world.

There were three cameras in the studio, each mounted on a huge metal pedestal that could be pushed silently across the floor with very little effort. Behind every camera stood a stationary cameraman like a statue. In the shadows, men with long poles padded about constantly moving fiercely bright lights which were suspended from the ceiling.

For some time no one took the slightest notice of me. Then a pretty girl, with long blond hair tied in a pony tail and a huge pair of headphones squeezing her ears together, smiled at me, introduced herself as Lizzie the floor-manager, and then frowned, peering forward in the gloom to study my face.

'Nasty boil you've got coming on there,' she said sympathetically. 'Never mind, we'll look after that.'

Feeling rather like a leper I followed her across the studio floor. What had she in mind? Plastic surgery?

Suddenly the corner of the studio was thrown into blinding light, like a biblical miracle, to reveal two hideous armchairs. In one of them, sparkling in the brightness, was a small vicar, staring straight ahead, as though in deep meditation, like some diminutive medieval pope upon a golden throne.

15

I sat down and smiled weakly at him.

'Hallo, in a moment you've got to interview me about my recent trip to South Africa,' he said in a slightly bored monotone. 'You must do it in exactly three minutes.'

Then something caught his eye and with sudden animation he leant forward eagerly.

'My, what a splendid boil you have coming there!' he said excitedly.

I wasn't feeling terribly confident by this stage, but before I had time to make a run for it Lizzie had appeared again and had plastered the offending boil with bucketfuls of make-up. Then, suddenly, we were off, and I began putting a series of unexciting questions to the glazed vicar about apartheid in South Africa and he began replying with the easy familiarity of a man who had been through it all a dozen times before.

That over, the vicar was plunged mysteriously into darkness again and I was led over to a desk from where I was expected to do my 'piece to camera'. This involved delivering a two-minute script directly to the camera and it put the fear of God into me.

I had written a ludicrous piece about how snuff can cure hayfever. It didn't matter that it was a load of old bull; what was important was that it gave me the opportunity to demonstrate something, rather than sit there like a stuffed marrow. This was a visual medium, after all, and plenty of snuff being pushed up nostrils and rubbed into gums might help disguise any fluffs I made in the script which, because no teleprompt was provided, I had memorised.

My heart beating like a bass drum I carefully perched my little box of snuff on the desk in front of me and, with a little wave from Lizzie behind the camera, I launched into it.

Things went smoothly until I was half-way through my piece. At this point, with my sweaty fingers trembling nervously, I opened the tin and picked up rather more snuff than I had intended — in fact a good deal more. The wretched stuff stuck to my fingers like glue, in great wadges.

I had no choice but to ram the lot up both nostrils. Manfully, I inhaled deeply.

At first, life seemed to have stopped completely. My mind went blank and I slowly realised that I had gone blind.

16

After what seemed like a fairly lengthy period I noticed the tips of my ears were tingling. Another curious sensation followed: heavy, fat tears began to roll down my cheeks, and with them my sight gradually returned, a wet, blurry mass of lights swimming about miles ahead somewhere. Then, as though a Bunsen burner was being held beneath my nose, I began to gasp for air, wheezing and coughing like an old church organ on the point of exploding.

*The TV audition.*

My senses slowly returned, so I plodded on, feverishly tipping quantities of snuff into my mouth and rubbing my gums like a maniac.

At last, fighting back the pain, I managed to get out the final words amidst a messy sea of burning brown saliva which dripped unceremoniously onto the lapels of my suit.

They loved it. Don said it was the funniest thing he had ever seen on television. Magic, he said. A few days later a contract dropped through the letterbox

• • •

The first filming assignment Don gave me was inauspicious: it was about toads. Now, I have never been a great lover of toads, but there are plenty of people about who are, so I suppose if you are a toad that is probably a good thing.

Anyhow, to be more precise, this was a film about the natterjack toad, and for those ignorant of such matters, the natterjack used to inhabit large areas of heathland all over Britain but has now become virtually extinct. In an attempt to reintroduce the species a team of toad enthusiasts had bred millions of the little horrors in laboratories so that they could release the most robust into the wild. It was the releasing exercise that Don wanted filming.

The little chaps were only about half-an-inch long, yet because there are so few of them about each was worth a small fortune on the black market (yes, there is a black market in toads). One of the scientists in charge of the operation was a vast, bearded man named Howell who reminded me of a picture in my school Bible of an irate Goliath. To describe him as obsessed with natterjack toads would be to underestimate things: the whole world apparently revolved about the ups and downs of the creature. He gave us stern instructions to walk about the heather in the release zone with extreme care as the toads were easy to step on by mistake. If one of us killed one, Goliath left us in no doubt that he would personally dismember the offender without trial. A strange smile of protective happiness passed across his face when he talked of the toads, like a lover: 'They have become my life, the symbol of my hopes and dreams,' he twittered on.

Since this was my first film I was very much in the hands of Ron the cameraman, a kind, flamboyant, experienced, infuriating fellow normally dressed in a flying-jacket. Today he was in a hurry to get away — Ron always seemed in a hurry to get away — and shortly after we arrived he suggested that I could explain much of the story in a short, introductory piece to camera on film.

Together we decided it would be quite effective if, as I was talking, I reached into my pocket, pulled out a natterjack toad, hold it to camera for a few moments, then watch it cheerfully jump away to its new life in the heather. Goliath, monitoring our every move, nearly had a fit when we suggested this but after a careful inspection of the inside of my pocket and a solemn promise that the selected

18

toad couldn't possibly come to any harm, he reluctantly agreed.

Just as we began shooting the sequence Goliath was distracted for a moment by one of his colleagues so he didn't see what happened, which was just as well.

This was Take One:

**Nigel**: (*to camera*) The interesting feature about this fascinating species of toad is that the friendly little fellow gets into all kinds of unusual places. Normally he likes to live in the heather at the base of trees, where he sleeps a good deal. But at night he becomes very active, hopping up the trees and out onto the branches. These charming, quite delightful creatures pop up all over the place ... hang on a moment, I think I can even feel one now in my pocket, cheeky chap!

*Nigel puts hand into pocket. Camera zooms in close on tightly-clenched fist. Nigel opens hand. On his palm there is a little mound of blood and toad-flesh. It is a dead natterjack toad.*

*Natterjack land.*

19

**Nigel:** (*to camera*)  Oh hell! I've squashed the little bugger!

I quickly hid the evidence in the heather as Ron and his soundman Peter began silently to rock with laughter and was just guiltily wiping the blood from my hand, rather like Lady Macbeth, when the giant suddenly reappeared, demanding: 'Everything all right over there?'

'Fine, fine,' I said quickly. 'I've let the tiny chap run off to play in the heather, happy as a sandpiper!'

A look of sheer contentment passed across his huge features.

'I do love those little toads,' he swooned.

● ● ●

The total lack of any kind of training in television reporting came as a surprise. Being thrown in at the deep end does have its advantages, but if you've been taught at least the basic rules of keeping afloat you will learn to swim much faster.

Yet much was expected. On Monday one is interviewing a man who has won the pools, on Tuesday a mother whose son has been murdered. One must coax emotion from people yet avoid accusations of intrusion into privacy. One must quickly master the highly technical process of filming yet make decisions about it without offending those colleagues involved. One must look perfect and speak perfectly; one must make sense to the lowest common denominator without putting off the highest; one must smile at abuse and sympathize with extremes. Yet because all is on public display, errors cannot be hidden easily and, anyway, there is usually no time to try. Are you weeping?

Nobody even bothered to show me around the building but after several days I discovered the reporters' room on the floor above the studio, which for three years was to be the centre of my universe.

If I had dreamed of television people working in luxurious offices I had woken up to reality. This was the dirtiest, scruffiest room I had ever stepped into. The curtains were hanging off the wall. The faded brown paint, stained a ghastly shade of yellow by generations of feverishly smoking journalists, was peeling and in places had dropped off in great ignominious blobs on the worn and coffee-stained carpet. Haphazardly arranged about the room were four desks — it was a pity there were five reporters — and on each, piled

20

high, were mountains of paper, ashtrays and coffee-cups. On one desk alone I counted 23 coffee-cups. On the shelves hanging on the walls there were rows of half-empty wine and whisky glasses, probably left over from the Roman Occupation, four London telephone directories and one *Who's Who*, a decade out of date. Pieces of old, broken typewriters lay where they had been thrown; on one wall there was a hatch which linked to the newsroom next door and from which, from time to time, a worried head would appear in search of an unemployed reporter. There never was one.

At the same time this shabby office was to become the exclusive clubroom for five of the most recognisable faces in the area. Regional television may only transmit its programmes to one small part of the country but within that it has an influence and a following far greater than most network programmes. As reporters, we were on peak-viewing television five nights a week; our regular presenters, Bruce and Jenni, were in vision more hours a week than any other personalities on television. They became regional television superstars.

Instant fame of this kind was also, naively, completely unexpected. A few weeks after I had entered the glittering world of television Don despatched me to film a charming story about a small village school in the heart of Dorset that was about to close. In the final week of the school's life the headmistress organised a summer picnic for all the children that was based almost exactly on the school's very first summer picnic in the week it was founded, nearly 200 years ago. Pupils, parents and staff all dressed up in 18th-century costume and, bathed in golden sunshine, as they played games and shared their picnic in the water meadows beside the village river, they looked quite magnificent.

Just as we had completed filming and were about to leave, one little boy, poking a piece of paper in my stomach, demanded my autograph. Now, when it comes to autographs and children, there is one basic rule which must be obeyed; you either refuse to sign any at all, or you sign the lot.

I was so overawed at his request that I immediately agreed. Within seconds, a rugby scrum of screaming children waving pieces of paper had formed around me. Realising, with growing horror, what I had let myself in for, I took a step back, tripped over a log,

*Autograph hunters.*

and fell flat on my back. Like the front line of a victorious army, the children surged forward, toppling over each other and forming a rising mound of bodies which not only pinned me to the ground but threatened to suffocate me, rather in the fashion employed so effectively by rioting Indians in their struggle for independence from the British Raj.

After a while a detachment of teachers arrived and began peeling away the bodies, with the efficiency of the Special Patrol Group, and once again I was able to see the light of day.

The upshot of all this was that without even consulting me, the teachers, anxious to maintain discipline, ordered that a queue be established for autographs. This formed very rapidly indeed and appeared, as I blinked in the bright sunlight, to stretch many miles away into the horizon. I had no option but to sit down on the grass and begin work; every child wanted at least one other autograph for his brother/sister/friend as well as his own, and, by the time the heat of the day had long since gone and the shadows were growing longer, I reckoned that I had signed my name nearly 600 times. I had lost all feeling in my right arm altogether; the fingers of my hand were numb and swollen, and the film crew, who had passed the time with a long game of poker, had to help me back to the car like a man who had suffered the ravages of a long and terrible torture.

Mind you, not all the attention I received was flattering. Some weeks after the mobbing incident, I went into a shop to buy a newspaper. As I walked through the door the old lady behind the till looked up and frowned at me, the lines of her face joining together like a squeezed sponge. Then all the lines vanished and she grew a deathly shade of pale; finally the colour returned to her cheeks and she smiled: 'I do beg your pardon, sir, but for one ghastly moment I thought you were that dreadful reporter on television.'

On another occasion the Marquis of Bath actually mistook me for a woman.

His Lordship was sitting in the green room, the hospitality suite, waiting to record an interview in the studio with a colleague of mine. On the television set in the corner of the room Naomi James was being interviewed about her voyage around the world.

As I walked in, my colleague turned to the Marquis of Bath and by way of conversation asked: 'Your Grace, have you ever met Naomi James, the round-the-world sailor?'

Lord Bath jumped to attention and strode over to meet me.

'Well done, well done indeed,' he beamed, grabbing my hand and shaking it violently. 'A very fine achievement.'

# 2

Five years earlier the exalted, magic world of television had seemed eons away. As a grubby cub reporter with inky fingers and shirt-collars that turned sharply up at the ends, as though warped by intense sunlight, my first journalistic posting was to a small weekly newspaper deep in green and leafy Sussex.

I had to write the obituaries.

I worked with a pretty, coolly efficient blonde girl called Marian. She and I together manned a tiny district office of the *Courier* newspaper in a village called Uckfield which was such a journalistic backwater that Marian derisively referred to it with the unsubtle addition of an initial letter 'F'. Our newly-painted office, windows emblazoned with old photographs of Uckfield School's Annual Sports Day and the Mayor meeting old folk at Christmas, stood in the High Street directly opposite the *Courier's* deadly rivals, the *Sussex Express*, similarly adorned. Marian's boyfriend was Kirbie, a vast Irishman and a reporter on the *Express* from whom, week after week, she would wheedle stories the *Express* staff were working on and so made sure that the *Courier* was never scooped.

As the *Express* had four reporters against our two, this earned Marian a reputation as an outstanding journalist and kept senior executives on both papers constantly puzzled.

Every Monday morning I had to ring the local undertaker for a list of all those in the village who had recently expired. With trembling fingers, I would then look up the names of the deceased in the telephone directory and ring their homes in the hope that their surviving loved ones could give me some details for an obituary. It was an odious task and probably one of the most difficult in the business; yet curiously, in most newspaper offices the obituaries are the responsibility of the most junior member of staff.

One name from that first week's undertaker's list is permanently engraved in my memory. The name is *Dunwoody* and even now when I hear of someone called Dunwoody a tremor whizzes down my spine.

The list informed me that the honest Mr Dunwoody had died quite suddenly of a heart-attack. Steeling myself I dialled his widow. This is what followed:

**Me**: (*in sonorous, pious tones*) I'm sorry to hear the bad news, Mrs Dunwoody.

**Mrs Dunwoody**: (*chirpily*) Ah well! Never mind! (*Pause*)

**Me**: We wanted to pay him a small tribute in the paper this week. Just a few paragraphs for his many friends and admirers to remember him by. (*Creepily*) Would you mind awfully giving me a few details about him?

**Mrs Dunwoody**: Mind? Why should I mind? He doesn't bloody well deserve it, though. (*Loud, snorting noise comes down telephone*) Lazy bugger. (*Long pause*)

**Me**: What sort of man was he?

**Mrs Dunwoody**: He *was* an 'ard-workin' member of society, he *was* respectable. (*Pause*) Not any more, though.

**Me**: No, I'm sorry.

**Mrs Dunwoody**: (*bitterly*) So am I. (*Pause*) Look, why don't you speak to the bugger yourself? I'll go and get him.

**Me**: Go and get him?

**Mrs Dunwoody**: Aye, he's only in the garden planting carrots.

No miracle, alas; I'd dialled the wrong Mr Dunwoody, who, it transpired, had just been sacked from his job, and the ensuing grovelling apologies must have been painful to hear.

I passed the first month or two at Uckfield pacing up and down the High Street in the hope that I would be the sole witness to some hugely dramatic act, such as the robbery of the local bank, the gunning down of the village postmaster by a gang of international terrorists, or even the storming of the Uckfield branch of the Halifax Building Society by the SAS. There was plenty of time to dream. Once Marian and I had supplied the newspaper's head office with our required amount of copy, the week's work was complete. There was nobody to keep an eye on us and even on a busy morning we

25

would retire to the Red Lion where Marian and Kirbie would canoodle diligently and I would gradually sink into a beery stupor. In the afternoon I would try to keep awake long enough to answer the telephone while Marian feverishly checked out all the information she had extracted from Kirbie.

At first life passed pleasantly enough, apart from the awful Monday morning obituary ordeal. I wrote an article about the arrival of the new village policeman, the owner of a fish-and-chip bar whose father had been killed by a jeep in Cyprus, and a former mental nurse who grew mushrooms in whisky; all riveting material that no doubt had my readers gasping with astonishment and counting off the seconds until the next edition of the paper dropped through the letterbox on Friday morning.

Even I had to admit that Uckfield didn't quite have the journalistic appeal of New York or Vietnam but at least it was a start.

One evening I was sitting in my bedsit munching a large marmalade sandwich when a story that was to dominate the headlines for months to come appeared on the television news.

The nanny of the Earl of Lucan had been found murdered. Lady Lucan had been discovered hysterical and covered in blood in a London pub. The earl himself was missing, and police forces throughout the world had been asked to help find him.

'The exact whereabouts of Lord Lucan remains a mystery,' announced the newsreader, as I leaned forward to turn up the volume with rapt attention. 'However, police activity is concentrated on the small village of —'

At this point a large map of Southern England appeared on the screen.

'— is concentrated on the village of Uckfield in Sussex.'

The marmalade sandwich slipped silently onto the floor.

'Uckfield is a small village between London and the South Coast and is the last place the missing earl was seen alive.'

Two place names suddenly appeared on the map, like magic. One was London in very small letters; the other, in very large letters, was Uckfield.

The next morning the village was alive with newsmen desperately in search of copy on a great story and starved of facts. It became clear that Lord Lucan had visited some friends in Uckfield after the murder and had later apparently driven on down to Newhaven before abandoning his car and disappearing.

Overnight Uckfield had become the most famous place in Britain.

As a national reporter chasing a provincial story your first port of call is always the local newspaper office in search of background, a typewriter and a telephone. Suddenly the humble district outpost of the *Courier* was swarming with more journalists, photographers and camera crews than I have ever seen, either before or since.

They all seemed to treat me with great respect as one by one they trotted in, grovelling to anyone who might possess an iota of information.

'Phillips, *Daily Mail*, how are you?'

'Farrell, *Courier*, fine. Take a seat. How can we help?'

The telephone rang incessantly. ITN, BBC, even NBC.

I'm sorry, NBC, you'll just have to wait,' I would say cockily. 'Now, who's next? Ah! Smithson, *Daily Express*, how can we help you old boy? Where do Lucan's friends live? Well, take the second left after the lights . . .' etc., etc.

No doubt they regarded me as an insufferable little squirt and made mental notes to warn their news editors to have the bargepole handy if ever I applied for a job, but they were all very polite and provided me with the most exciting few days I had had in years.

I made a point of ringing all my friends.

One by one they faithfully asked how I was coping with the new job.

'Oh, fine, fine,' I would reply casually. 'I'm actually a bit busy at present, I'm afraid. Lot on.'

'What are you working on?'

'Lucan case is taking up most of the time, don't you know.'

My social standing zoomed up to new and heady heights. My mother thought I'd be in Fleet Street within weeks.

Gradually, tragically, the excitement died down. Every conceivable angle on the story was exhausted. Uckfield subsided into its awful normality.

Just after the last national reporter had left our office, never to return, the telephone on my desk burst once again into life.

'Farrell, *Courier*,' I chanted wearily.

It was my shorthand teacher, demanding an explanation for my absence at her last lesson.

*'Farrell,* Courier. *How can we help?'*

Journalism had been a last resort. For a year after leaving school I hovered dangerously close to becoming a doctor and the fact that I was kicked out of medical school is something for which every ill person should be eternally grateful.

The trouble was that I came from an incorrigibly medical family. My great-grandfather was a doctor. My uncle was a doctor. My father was a doctor. My brother was a doctor. I didn't want to let the side down so I decided to be a doctor, too. The fact that the sight of blood makes me go wobbly at the knees was neither here nor there.

I managed to survive one disastrous year at St Bartholomew's Hospital Medical School in London. Unleashed in the big city alone at the tender age of 17, I spent 10 per cent of my time falling in love with every girl I met, 10 per cent seeing every new show in town, and 80 per cent drinking in the medical students' bar at the hospital, which closed only when there were no customers still standing upright.

I'm afraid my studies hardly got a look in. Dazzled by the new liberal academic atmosphere where one was no longer beaten for being lazy, I didn't go to a single lecture for two weeks. This was unfortunate. During that first fortnight the basic scientific principles and terminology upon which the whole year's work depended were explained. Consequently, simple scientific words like 'neutron', 'atomic weight', 'affinity' and 'negative electron' remained without any meaning at all and the entire academic year passed me by as a total mystery.

It was the first year exams which found me out, of course. I couldn't understand the questions, let alone provide any answers.

What I didn't really appreciate at the time was that we were being taught basic physics by one of the world's most eminent physicists, a man who helped work on the Manhatten Project to develop the Bomb during the Second World War and who had since thrown himself into medical research. He was held in high esteem by the international scientific community and it must have been the philanthropist within him that made him sacrifice four or five hours a week of his precious hospital time to teach us raw novices the rudiments of elementary physics.

I went chirpily into the first year exam confident that I would be able to bluff my way through it as I had every other exam in the past. When I read the question paper I immmediately felt a curious tingling sensation in the pit of my stomach which informed me I was on the verge of panic. The entire paper was an enigma. What made it worse was that within seconds everyone else was busily scribbling away furiously, like rotten swots. All our exams were held in huge, cold laboratories and with a name like Farrell I was high on the alphabetical list and had to sit near the front, right under the nose of the invigilator. As the minutes went by he kept giving me odd little glances as though he was sitting close to a dangerous lunatic. Behind me, like a horrible chorus, came the endless scratch, scratch, scratch of pens on paper as my fellow students poured out an interminable stream of knowledge.

I looked again at the exam paper. There was only one question I could conceivably tackle during the next three-and-a-half hours, and it was this: 'Describe in some detail the physiological changes the pilot of a fast fighter aircraft might undergo during high-speed aerobatics.' By chance, a few weeks before, I had read Sir Douglas Bader's famous biography *Reach For the Sky* in which it had been explained that Bader could fly a much tighter turn than his colleagues because he had no legs. Centrifugal force pushes the pilot's blood away from his head and down towards his legs during a turn — the longer the legs, the greater the danger of passing out. A legless pilot was therefore at a great advantage.

With this solitary fact at my disposal, I set about writing an essay which, in the absence of anything else to fill the time, turned out to be a short history of the Second World War. With the Bader

*The medical exam.*

incident the climax to the piece, I launched into a dramatic and detailed analysis of the aerial tactics of both the Luftwaffe and the RAF during the early, critical years of the conflict. I knew that the good professor was Polish and in the hope of winning him over I made a point of praising the extreme gallantry of the Polish airmen, defiant in the face of the evil Nazi jackboot, etc., etc. At the end of the exam I sat back with some satisfaction, and neatly piled up the 16 sheets of foolscap paper which I felt sure put forward a convincing argument proving that the principles behind the whole Luftwaffe strategy were fundamentally unsound.

A few days later the exam results were pinned on one of the corridor noticeboards in the physics department. I got zero, a fact which caused great merriment amongst my colleagues and earned me free drinks in the bar for nearly a week. When my papers were returned I noticed that the professor, instead of writing a constructive comment, had simply put a sad little question mark at the end of my efforts.

It was only months afterwards that I came to regard what I had done with fading amusement and a growing sense of shame.

At least in the biochemistry practical I made an attempt, however pathetic, to prove I was a budding Christian Barnard.

We were each provided with a live locust in a glass dish. The exam paper specified that this must be pinned down on a block of wood, its stomach wall sliced open, and its intestines dipped into a small bowl of chemical to test their enzyme balance (whatever that was). This whole ghastly operation had to be carried out whilst the poor creature was still alive because, the paper informed me, once dead the enzyme balance would dramatically change. As it was squirming about in my fingers, I did what I could to pin down the wretched creature firmly on the block. Just as I was hauling out its intestines, the locust suddenly wriggled free and flew off. Fighting back the urge to be sick, I watched in horror as it flew across the laboratory with its entrails trailing out behind it, dripping blood all over the other student's exam papers. Eventually it reached a wall, and the exam had to be temporarily abandoned as we all tried to catch the thing as it began to crawl up onto the ceiling in its final death throes.

At the end of term I was summoned to the Dean's office and very politely asked if I had ever considered an alternative occupation, preferably as far away from London as possible.

From Medical School I applied for the job of ticket reservation clerk at BOAC. The interview was a fiasco, culminating in my being asked the following question: 'If an aeroplane flew from London to Singapore in a straight line, over which countries would it pass?' I got as far as the Channel Islands and my mind went blank.

Then I worked as a travel agent. This ended when I booked a

31

passenger to Australia on a flight which didn't exist. When he arrived at Heathrow, tears rolling down his cheeks as he bade a long farewell to his large family, he was told that he would have to wait 24 hours for his flight.

'That can't be right,' he protested, with touching confidence in my abilities. 'The man in the travel agency personally booked me on a flight that is to leave later this morning.'

Eventually he was convinced. He returned 24 hours later and just as he was about to embark on the aircraft to Australia, he was asked for the innoculation documents for his planned stopover in Singapore.

'I don't need innoculation documents,' he protested again. 'The man in the travel agency said you don't need innoculation certificates for this trip.

Another 24 hours later he finally made it on board. I never discovered if he had a pleasant flight; the vehement letter of complaint didn't go into that kind of detail.

Finally, I hitch-hiked to Italy with an old mate. Our money ran out within a few weeks, and for the next three months we were constantly teetering on the verge of starvation. We tried to get work, any work, washing-up, or even cleaning out the awful public latrines in Rome. The employers all demanded to see our work permits. The British Embassy no longer issued work permits because Britain had just joined the Common Market and such

*Roman interlude.*

permits were no longer necessary. The employers refused to believe this, so we were reduced to stealing scraps of food from the plates of affluent society restaurant-goers. Cigarettes were begged from strangers in the street. We became like parasitic grubs, ekeing out an unsavoury survival from the waste or kindness of others.

All in all, an excellent training for a career in journalism.

When I arrived home, destitute, penniless and suffering from scurvy, a respectable job was suddenly quite attractive. I wrote to the head office of the local paper, the *Courier*, and was told to submit a short account of a local event of my choice. I went along to a poetry reading at which the author Kingsley Aims was appearing. Mr Amis was very kind and gave me a charming interview sprinkled lavishly with clever and witty quotes. Most of these I rewrote in narrative as my own; the *Courier* hired me and the distant outpost of Uckfield was the result.

• • •

Life with Marian was easy and agreeable. Her talent and competence quickly smoothed over any difficulties we encountered in the office; and thrown together all day, every day, she spent a great deal of time clucking about her protégé like an old hen, checking my spelling and apologising to irate members of the public for my mistakes. Being clucked about by a pretty blonde dynamo hour after hour is a soothing, very pleasant way of passing the time, and after only a few weeks I found myself a little in love with her.

From time to time we bumped into the harsher side of reality and often this came as quite a shock. Marian took me to a neighbouring Magistrates Court for the first time and the proceedings left me empty and depressed. The Clerk to the Court was a pompous, bumptious little official who seemed to take positive delight in humiliating both defendant and solicitors alike. The magistrates, nicely groomed, either possessed a slightly puzzled air or were dozing off. The air was heavy and stagnant, broken only by the mournful comings and goings of those requiring punishment.

The first case involved a youth of my own age who had stolen money from the garage where he was employed. He was brought up to the dock from the cells which were immediately beneath the court itself. The sound of the cell door being unlocked and the footsteps climbing the stone staircase into a court waiting to pass judgement in grim silence was like something straight out of the Middle Ages. I couldn't see the lad's face but he was standing so close I could have reached out and touched him. I could hear his fast, heavy breathing; his hands, clasped together behind his back, squirmed incessantly, the nervous damp fingers locking and unlocking over and over again.

The lad pleaded guilty and with evident glee the Clerk announced that this was his second offence. The Magistrates nudged each other awake and entered a short, muffled discussion, after which the lady chairman of the Bench announced that the lad was to be sent to prison for six months. As she spoke, the hands a few feet away from me went into a spasm of activity.

That appalling silence descended again as the youth was led away, back down those awful steps, back into the locked cells. The Clerk, pausing for dramatic effect, waited until the sound of the key grating in the lock had died away before announcing the next case.

The memory of those tortured hands haunted me for months.

A few weeks later I was sitting at my desk doodling and secretly admiring Marian, busy on the other side of the room, when the telephone rang. Marian answered it and as she stood there listening intently she suddenly blanched.

Marian put down the phone and said: 'There's been a double murder.'

At first I thought she was joking; but she was out of that office so fast that I had no choice but to gallop after her and leap into her car as it picked up speed down the High Street.

We had no difficulty finding the house. There was a small posse of stony-faced policemen pacing up and down outside, like lionesses protecting their young from marauders. Marian knew them all, of course, and as I stood there nervously hopping from one foot to another watching her marching off to talk to them, I began to see why some editors always send their most attractive female reporters to cover difficult cases like this. Marian extracted the complete story in about 23 seconds.

She explained it so matter-of-factly; I was shocked at her icy efficiency.

34

'Mother very depressed after husband left her. Last night went berserk, strangled both her children.'

Just like that.

I looked again at the policemen, posted like grim sentries outside the ordinary little bungalow in this ordinary residential road lined with tall, sycamore trees. It was hard to take in.

Marian was pulling at my sleeve.

'You see the house next door?' she asked impatiently. 'Go and chat 'em up.'

'Chat 'em up?' I echoed, appalled.

'Get a bit of background about the family. Did they know the murdered children well? Ask for old photographs.'

'Are you serious?'

'Get on with it!'

I walked over to the house as slowly as I could, praying that if I played for time long enough there would be some divine intervention which would prevent me having to knock on the door. Perhaps there'd be an earthquake; a modest thunderbolt would do.

I looked over my shoulder. Marian, like a Greek goddess, was pointing at the house, a stern, unbending statue.

I took a deep breath, rapped on the door, and racked my brain for a way of introducing myself which wouldn't sound too dreadful in such circumstances.

Perhaps they'd be out.

I waited no more than a few seconds and was about to make a dash for freedom when, to my horror, the door creaked open and a middle-aged woman, with one of the most beautiful faces I have ever seen, appeared like a vision before me.

A gentle smile was playing on her lips.

'Hello, I'm ... er ... I'm sorry to, er, hear about your next-door neighbours ... er ... frightful business and all that ... frightful ... er ...'

I blathered on like a moron for a few minutes while the woman listened politely. Eventually, I dried up. When I thought about it I was surprised she hadn't slammed the door in my face.

At last she said: 'You're from the local paper?'

I nodded.

'Come in.'

She sat me down, her eyes sparkling and that knowing smile never far away, and made me coffee.

'This must be very difficult for you,' she said soothingly, and I said yes, it was, unable to take my gaze from her face.

'I knew them very well, you know. Shall I tell you?'

I nodded again, like an idiot.

'Shouldn't you be writing this down?'

Feverishly, I searched through my pockets. I had left my notebook in the office.

The woman went to her desk and returned with paper and a pen. Then she began to talk: I scribbled.

Ten minutes later I had the story sewn up.

I didn't want to leave but the woman pointed out that Marian would be wondering what had happened to me so reluctantly I thanked her and said goodbye.

'Are these of any interest?' she asked just as I was leaving.

They were a bundle of photographs she had taken of the dead children only a week before. 'A nasty business,' she said, shaking her head sadly.

Marian was very impressed. She gave me a slightly odd look from the corner of her eye and told me she had obviously underestimated my abilities. I agreed, enthusiastically.

We hurried on to find a telephone box to 'phone Head Office. When, at last, we found one it was occupied by a reporter from one of our rival local papers. He was jabbering away at the rate of knots.

'He'll be hours,' said Marian.

'What's he doing?'

'He's 'phoning round the story to all the national papers. He'll also be calling local radio, television and the BBC in London. This morning's little murder will have earned him quid or so.'

I peered in through the misty glass of the call box. The reporter, still chattering away, grinned and gave me the thumbs-up sign.

It all seemed slightly unreal.

By the time we returned to the scene the television crews and already arrived. Reporters and photographers were buzzing up and down the street like bees around a honey-pot. Astonished passers-by were set upon and interrogated; everything that moved was photographed or filmed.

This quiet cul-de-sac had begun to take on the appearance of a merry carnival. The camera crews were greeting each other like old friends, standing around in small groups exchanging stories and telling jokes. Marian was being embraced by a young television reporter whose face I instantly recognised. He looked a slippery eel on the screen; in the flesh he looked more slippery and eel-like than ever.

'All I can say, dear, is thank God for this,' I heard him tell her, waving an arm theatrically towards the scene of the ghastly double murder. 'Without it Jeremy would have had *real* problems filling tonight's programme.'

I began to wonder what kind of profession I had entered.

It was only after life had returned to its usual draining torpidity that I realised that the double murders and Lucan scandals had probably used up Uckfield's quota of important news for the next millenium. The place retreated to the comfort and security of hibernation and my desk was once again piled high with the details of the two phenomena without which local rural newspapers would collapse: weddings and obituaries. There are only a limited number of ways of describing a person's marriage or funeral without greatly offending their loved ones and you don't need to be Dickens or Tolstoy to discover what they are.

I began to see why journalism has one of the highest percentage of alcoholics of any profession. Extracting information is best done in a social atmostphere and a drop of this or that can usually help. The trouble is that for most journalists — so used to working in superlatives — moderation is an unfashionable word.

When nobody in town had died or been married Marian dispatched me on visits to nearby villages and hamlets with instructions not to return until I had found at least half-a-dozen stories. These trips normally got off the mark with a visit to the vicarage. The vicar, anxious to plug his parish news and, with luck, catch the eye of the bishop, would produce enough sherry to top-up a reservoir or two. Then, after a speedy noggin with one of the local farmers or the area's National Farmer's Union rep. it was off for a liaison with that other lynchpin of rural life, the landlord of the village pub. Here enough deliciously scandalous gossip to fill several volumes of the *News of the World* would be exchanged;

unfortunately so much beer was involved that by the time I was ejected in a happy haze at closing-time little was retained. Indeed, recalling how to get back to the office was often an ordeal, and even this went awry on occasions.

In the evenings, nursing a sore head and trying to stay awake, I would sit through hours of parish councils, or meetings of trades groups and ratepayers associations, and at the end of the day I would return to my bedsit in dejection. Every passing week, it seemed, increased my chances of staying in Uckfield for eternity. What's more, there seemed little chance of prizing Marian away from Kirbie, and the fact that he was Uckfield's version of Deep Throat left me little hope for the future.

Heavily disguising my almost total lack of experience, I wrote a long letter to the editor of a big daily evening newspaper based in Southampton and much to my surprise he agreed to see me. He turned out to be very far from the image of a brash, shirt-sleeved egomaniac equipped with green eye-shade and chewing gum that I had imagined; instead he was a very quiet, gentlemanly man with a pointed little beard on the end of his chin like Philip of Spain. He seemed to be more nervous of me than I of him; and after hearing about how, single-handed, I had been mercilessly hunting Lord Lucan, and how my fearless reporting of the double murder tragedy had shocked and shattered an entire community, he politely offered me a job rather in the manner of someone who believed I would be mortally offended if he did not.

I was excited at the prospect of working on a regional newspaper with a big circulation which not only carried local but national and international news as well — and not once a week, but with two or three editions every day. Armed with a letter which confirmed that I would start on the paper's district office in the heart of the New Forest a few miles to the west of Southampton, my bank manager agreed to a loan and, in celebration, I decided to buy my first motor-car.

My choice of vehicle was disastrous.

The best I could afford was small, seventh-hand Citroen 2CV saloon which had been imported from Belgium. Its great advantage was that it had an engine the size of a lawn-mower and could thus travel at about 70 miles to the gallon. Its great disadvantage was that it was on the point of total disintegration.

It was only several days after I had bought the car that I realised most of the chassis had completely rusted away. Everything was held together by the roof structure; if I had to brake suddenly the whole car would bend under the strain and, much to my consternation, along with that of passers-by, all four doors would open simultaneously. In fact, as the days passed, a hole developed in the brake pipes so that the only way I *could* stop was to pump the footbrake like a maniac for several seconds until the pressure had built up and the car came to an abrupt and absolute halt. Such was the ensuing strain on things that the phenomenon of all four doors opening at once thus became fairly routine.

Furthermore, the car had a roll-back canvas sun-roof which was anchored by two steel bolts at the front. These had also rusted. Whenever I passed a large lorry travelling in the opposite direction there would be a fearful ripping sound, the bolts would give and I would find myself with only sky above me and the canvas roof flapping madly like a sail behind.

It's not over yet, I'm afraid. The two headlights were screwed to

*The first Farrellmobile.*

39

a metal bar attached to the front of the bonnet and this, too, had rusted. After a few minutes driving — less if the road was particularly bumpy — the bar would work loose and the headlights would gradually begin to point upwards. This was particularly alarming if I was driving on a dark, unlit road; at first all before me was perfectly illuminated; then, as the lights moved up, the road was plunged into blackness and all I could see was the top of the hedge; finally, all that was lit were the peaks of passing tall trees and any low-flying aircraft in the area.

On one occasion, with the headlights pointing vertically like searchlights into the dark night sky, a juggernaut passed me at speed. With a whoosh! the roof disappeared behind and, after violent pumping of the brake, I came to a sudden stop and all four doors opened.

Just as I was extracting myself from the wretched thing a police motorcyclist appeared. At first, the poor man thought the car had been blown up by a bomb. Then, when he finally brought himself to accept my explanation, he booked me for every offence under the sun. I thought this vaguely unfair. Instead of booking me, he should really have been congratulating me on my great driving skill in being able to master such an unconventional machine. The Order for Outstanding Motoring would have been more appropriate.

Nevertheless, the car was all I could afford. Loaded up with my belongings from the bedsit, I kissed Marian a tearful farewell, waved goodbye to Uckfield for ever, and, driving very slowly indeed and in broad daylight, I set off South.

# 3

The desire to impress my new newspaper by arriving early for work on my first day was thwarted when the confounded car burst into flames en route to the New Forest.

I was cheerfully rolling along, with a merry whistle on my lips and the joyful sounds of the countryside filling my ears, when huge clouds of dense grey smoke began billowing from the engine. By now I had become so used to the idiosyncracies of this remarkable vehicle that they no longer alarmed me; and as I was only a few miles away from the office and the end of my journey, I decided to plough on regardless. Unfortunately the smoke became so thick that I could see no more than a few centimetres past the windscreen, which was rather like flying an aircraft in dense cloud. Had I been able to observe their reaction, passers-by would no doubt have stopped and stared, open-mouthed, at the sight of a small, mobile inferno whizzing through the gentle hills and valleys of the beautiful New Forest leaving a trail of charred and blackened trees in its wake.

Eventually, with an audible groan, the car conked out. After a few minutes the smoke subsided and, making sure that the car was left unlocked in the forlorn hope that some idiot would steal it so that I could claim insurance, I abandoned it on the side of the road and began walking.

This meant that I was very late indeed for work.

To my surprise and slight disappointment the newspaper's New Forest office was even smaller and uglier than the Uckfield equivalent. I suppose I had expected a huge, glistening black block towering above the pavement with at least twelve stories and a man in a smart uniform greeting the reporter's cars as they arrived; instead here was a grey little 1930s shop, with old peeling paint and several tiles missing from its roof, dwarfed by the butcher's next door. Inside there was a tiny wooden counter where the public placed small ads. Behind that stood an ancient, rickety printing press on which the shop's three middle-aged ladies would add the Stop

Press news and the latest racing results to the stacks of papers which arrived already printed up from the main office in Southampton every afternoon.

I introduced myself and one by one the three ladies shook me by the hand, each laughing and smiling with a radiant cheerfulness that quite took me by surprise. They chattered away with such astonishing joviality that I assumed something wonderful had just happened to them, like winning the pools or being offered free holidays in Barbados; it was only as the days passed did I realise that they were always like this, rattling away to each other at the rate of knots, giggling and chuckling and frequently piercing the peace with shrieks of uncontrollable laughter. This was a little disconcerting at first.

I didn't realise it then but on that first meeting I must have presented a formidable sight, covered in engine oil and soot, with my hair standing straight up in spikes like a cartoon character who had been given a bomb to hold seconds before it had gone off. I don't know whether my appearance added to the general hilarity but we all seemed to get along famously and by the time we had all stopped laughing I felt much more optimistic.

At the back of the office there was a wobbly wooden staircase leading to a squat little room that looked as though it had been thrown onto the back of the building as an apologetic after-thought. This was the reporters' room, equipped with one small desk and two even smaller chairs, which left just enough room for a rusty old heater and standing-room for one child/dwarf. From the window was a spectacular panoramic view of a car park.

One of the chairs was always occupied by Keith, my new young boss, an extremely experienced reporter, with an eternally youthful face and the patience of a saint. He had once distinguished himself in the local magistrates court by managing to rugger-tackle the accused who had tried to make a run for it upon hearing the unpleasant details of his conviction; ever after Keith was kept well abreast of all the local news and often offered little exclusives by a grateful police force. Over the years he had developed a superb network of contacts so that he knew more about the New Forest than any other single living person. He was often known, for example, to arrive on the scene of a fire before the fire brigade, which of course enabled him to pick up several useful quotes from those trapped in burning rooms before they were rescued.

Keith was also extremely conscientious and, apart from looking after me like a father, he was stickler for accuracy. This was a particularly commendable quality in the light of the horrendous printing errors the newspaper would produce day after day. His work was edited and printed with so many mistakes that the sense of many of his stories was completely lost. Places and names would be mysteriously switched; complete words would change, so that 'tomorrow' would become 'yesterday', 'Friday' would suddenly reappear as 'Monday', and, on one glorious occasion, 'engine driver' became 'elephant driver' which since there is a severe shortage of elephants in the New Forest gave his story an unexpected, global significance. Each morning, when we 'phoned over our stories to Head Office, Keith would check and recheck with the copy-typist that there was no mistake; every afternoon the stories would appear in the paper, lacerated, and quite a challenge to understand.

Nevertheless, Keith ploughed on manfully, turning out in the middle of a winter's night to cover the search for a child lost out on the heathland, or a cow being rescued from a swimming-pool, with the stoicism that some of the desk-chained clockwatchers at Head Office never appreciated.

His conscientiousness sometimes led to unfortunate consequences. During my first week, for example, Keith took me to cover a wine convention at a very expensive local hotel. Inside the main hotel ballroom stood a row of trestle tables, each lined with exotic bottles beautifully laid out for tasting. On the extreme left of the room there were the very sweet, white wines; on the extreme right, several hundred bottles later, the very full-bodied red wines. I had already gathered that Keith was not a drinking man, so I was duly surprised when he came out with the immortal words: 'The only correct way to write a proper story about this, sunshine, is to jolly well taste every single one.'

I did what I could to stop him, but with great determination and armed with a notebook and pen, he marched off and set about the white wines with a vengeance, without, I observed with growing alarm, making any use of the elegant silver spittoons provided.

Within only a few minutes, Keith was well down the line of bottles. He had begun to weave his way ahead; and as he worked his path through the dry whites towards the rosé, I noticed his right hand never left the edge of the table, rather like troops on night exercise blindly following a rope up the side of a mountain.

*Keith looks upon the grapes . . .*

By the time he reached the Bordeaux his young, healthy, pink complexion had turned a bright puce, rather like an over-ripe tomato. He was giggling quietly to himself.

Five minutes later, satiated, he strode over to me and announced it was time to leave. He spoke without any hint of a slur, and without another word he walked over to his car and we both climbed in. Keith then put his car into what he thought was reverse gear, and looking purposefully over his left shoulder so that he could see exactly where he was going, he drove the car straight into a large ditch a few yards in front of us.

I knew from this moment that we would get on well together.

Life soon formed a comfortable, familiar routine: up early in the morning to check the overnight stories with the police, the fire brigade, the coastguards and the ambulance service; 'phone them over to the Southampton office for the afternoon editions; then out to court or district council meetings. In the afternoons Keith and I would squash ourselves back into our tiny, cold office and bang out the morning's stories on a pair of old typewriters, gazing out into the dismal, grey car park for inspiration and trying not to be distracted by the gales of laughter that floated up every few minutes from the shop-front below.

There was one duty, however, that my new boss was reluctant to perform. This he smartly passed on to his inexperienced deputy with what, in hindsight, I regard as indecent haste.

At first I didn't realise what I had let myself in for. Like all the best-laid traps, it came in disguised form, just as Keith was struggling into a coat one evening to go home. Looking at me with an innocent, helpful expression, Keith asked: 'Fancy a free night out, sunshine?'

What would you have said? Of course I nodded thankfully, and the wily old fox passed me an envelope. Before I had a chance to open it he was out of the door and gone, shouting up as he trotted down the stairs and into the darkness, 'Knock out a few paragraphs as a review for tomorrow's paper if you like.'

Inside the envelope were two tickets, not, as I had gratefully expeced, to the casino in Bournemouth or a strip club in Southampton, but to the local amateur dramatic who-dun-it at the village hall. Now this in itself, though disappointing, was not a disaster; after all, I hadn't anything else to do that evening. The disaster was to follow.

Now just in case, dear reader, you are ever in the unfortunate position of having to review such a production, remember that in rural life at least the amateur dramatic group is probably the most important and powerful pressure group in the community. It is normally made up of the more influential members of society for whom acting is a jolly jape, a chance to consume large quantities of alcohol and a perfect excuse for being late home at night. A pat on the back in the local paper review is a vital ingredient to the success of the ritual.

I had always been vaguely interested in the theatre and as I set off that fateful evening I resolved that my review would sparkle with literary promise. Unfortunately the production was quite pathetic: lines were forgotten, prompts shouted out, often during genuine dramatic pauses, props didn't work, bits of scenery fell off. At the beginning of act three the carefully tape-recorded sound effects went completely out of synchronisation with the action, so that everyone — actors, backstage staff and audience — was thrown into total confusion. Cars were heard to drive up to the front door long after their occupants had arrived on stage; telephones would start to ring long after they had been answered, etc., etc.

I wrote a brilliant, damning review and 'phoned it over to the office before Keith arrived for work.

It took several days to work out why I was being shunned in public life. Councillors ignored me during coffee at council meetings; shopkeepers refused to pass the time of day; the wives of local business men crossed the road when they saw me walking towards them.

Keith made low, whistling sounds when he read what I had written. 'You all start off the same, sunshine, but you'll never write another review like this.' Then he chuckled softly. 'Mind you, this is a real humdinger!'

Just as he had said this, the sustained laughter from below suddenly stopped. There was a short silence followed by very angry shouting. Keith disappeared at speed and returned a few moments later.

'That was Howard Mulligans, the churchwarden, and he's not very pleased.'

'Why not?'

'He was responsible for the sound effects in last night's play. Apparently the phrase: "rambling cacophany that brought tears to the eyes ..." hit him where it hurt, sunshine.'

I winced.

Keith grinned. 'Don't worry, I told him you were out on a story.'

I would have been happy never to write another review but Keith, who hated them even more than me, insisted I do the lot. Gradually I became adept at describing performances in glowingly average terms. An entire vocabulary of totally inoffensive words was brought into use. Thus, a production was 'stimulating' with a 'varied' set, an 'interesting' musical score, a 'notable' leading man with 'consistent' back-up from a cast equipped with 'unusual' costumes and an 'honest' interpretation from the director.

After several months of sitting through a string of truly appalling efforts I came across that rare phenomenon, a local amateur dramatic play that was actually quite good. This so took me by surprise that I raved about it in my review; being able to write something positive about a production was a sweet luxury. As a result the company offered me one of the leading parts in their next production, and so guaranteed themselves rave reviews for life. By the time the play was staged I had got to know all the reporters from the other local papers and I made it abundantly clear that good reviews were expected all round. Some of the reviews I even wrote myself. Thus you-know-who came out of it with flying colours, e.g. 'In a cast that positively sparkled with fun, Nigel Farrell took the colours with an outstanding performance . . ., Nigel Farrell led the laughter . . . . the biggest applause was for Nigel Farrell . . . etc., etc.'

As word got about of my power and influence, I found myself being offered all the best parts in plays throughout the area. I was bribed by endless free meals and for several weeks never even had to buy a drink. Life became quite rosy. I considered hiring an agent.

Like many of those who achieve rapid stardom, however, my decline came suddenly, and was the result of excess alcohol. One of the local amateur dramatic groups had made the mistake of staging a long series of medieval mystery plays which attempted, in one session, to dramatise the story of the Bible. You will agree that this was an ambitious project not made any easier by the fact that most of it was in archaic language understandable only to those with a Ph.D. or above in medieval English.

The production was to be held in the open air, as part of a garden party, and it began at 2.35 pm, just after the pubs had closed. After guarantees of superb reviews I had been given the plum part of the first shepherd in the nativity sequence and I'm afraid with my colleagues the second and third shepherds I had consumed liberal quantities of luncheon refreshment. During the play the three shepherds had to be seen sipping wine from jugs they carried slung

47

*The singing shepherds.*

to their waists. In a misguided attempt at authenticity, the director had made the elementary mistake of ordering real wine — in fact, a great deal of real wine.

We went on stage having decided that the play had become desperately slow, boring and turgid and needed a little 'livening up.' First of all the second shepherd departed from the script just before the arrival of Archangel Gabriel and started telling filthy jokes instead. The third shepherd began distributing free wine to anyone in the audience who wanted it — and some who didn't — and the first shepherd tried to get things moving with a sing-song that got underway with 'She'll Be Coming Round The Mountain' and deteriorated into 'The Hairs On Her Dickie-Di-Do'.

Even at the start of the play, Chapter One of Genesis, there had never been a huge audience, and most of them had begun to drift away to other amusements at the garden party well before Deuteronomy, although a few religious diehards had stuck it out into the New Testament. During the nativity sequence, however, even these moved quickly away, and by the end of the play our audience consisted of no more than three disabled people in wheelchairs who had been abandoned by their helpers and had no choice but to see the thing through.

After that, despite reviews which described how brilliantly the nativity sequence had breathed new life into this godly celebration etc., etc., word got around that the first shepherd was a liability with alcoholic tendencies and that perhaps after all it was better to put up with poor reviews.

● ● ●

Keith taught me that there was a story to be found almost anywhere. If he sent me to cover an evening meeting of a small parish council in the New Forest, which perhaps was made up of three or four members and lasted no more than half an hour, I was expected to produce two or three stories at least. Instead of nodding gently off at the back of the hall and then simply adjourning to the pub, I was forced to keep thinking, all the time searching for something amusing, something important, something informative to say. It was a time which stood me in good stead later in television when, out with a large film crew costing hundreds of pounds an hour, to return to the office without a story was considered the ultimate unprofessional act.

One morning Keith bounced up the stairs to our office, stuck his head around the door and said: 'Grab your coat, sunshine, I've had a tip from a mate in the Social Services department. It could be a good one.'

We in turn tipped off our regular local freelance photographer and drove off quickly to a small estate in an outlying village. Outside one of the houses stood an ambulance; about a hundred yards further on two policemen, rubbing their hands and stamping their feet to keep warm, held back a small crowd of children.

Keith wandered casually over and talked to one of the constables for a moment, then returned shrugging his shoulders.

'Wait and see.'

This was unusual. Keith knew every policeman in the district — he'd been to school with most of them — yet he'd been given no hint of what was happening.

We waited for about 20 minutes. The estate was right on the edge of the New Forest, and way ahead, past the small groups of ponies with ribs showing from a hard winter, enclosures of trees and huge tracts of untouched heathland lay stretched out to the horizon. Thin sheets of morning mist drifted over the streams and the lower, wet marshes; in the distance shimmered the dim outline of the hills of the Isle of Wight.

Suddenly people started to move and the front door of the little house swung open.

Out stepped two extraordinary little figures. They were like pygmies, bent and wizened, their frail forms wrapped in blankets and supported by an ambulanceman and a social worker as they hobbled out into the road. They were both jet black — not the black of a negro, but of years of dirt and grime and neglect.

It was an amazing sight.

When the ambulance had driven them both away into care, we were able to piece together the story. Over the last 20 years neither the old man nor his wife had stepped out of the house. Each week food supplies and a little money had been passed through a window by an old relative and neighbour. It appeared the couple had never changed their clothes and never cleaned the house. Now they had finally been forced to give up their fight for total independence through old age.

My first thought was that the move into care would probably kill them.

It was a horrifying story and on the way back to the office I chattered away excitedly to Keith about how it could end up as a page lead in one of the national papers or even a Sunday. 'With a good picture the *News of the World* may pay hundreds of pounds for a story like this. The local newsagency in Bournemouth will move in and syndicate the story all over the world. I could be worth a fortune.'

For several minutes Keith said nothing. We drove in silence past the great, overhanging oak trees which had made the New Forest famous. Some young deer poked their heads gingerly over a fence then raced away as we sped past.

'We write two sentences recording the fact that they have been taken into care,' said Keith at last. 'No pictures, no details. I'm not humiliating them still further.'

Suddenly I felt a fool for suggesting it.

● ● ●

Keith and I quickly became good friends.

As a diversion to the long, dreary hours we spent huddled in our cold little office banging out stories, we invented a game which provided us with hours of amusement in the evenings and which lent us a certain notoriety throughout the area.

At the end of each working day, the three ladies down below in the shop, still chuckling away, placed all the unsold copies of the newspaper in a rack on the wall, underneath which was a large sign asking anyone who wanted a paper to take one and place fivepence through the letterbox.

Only a very few, honest people actually deposited the full fivepence, of course. Some, if we were lucky, dropped in one or two pennies, but most left buttons, bottle-tops or stones, shoved through for the benefit of passers-by.

On winter's evenings, if we were bored, we would shut up shop at 5.30 as usual and turn out all the lights. Our three ladies, trying desperately to suppress the giggles, would then crouch down out of sight under the letterbox whilst Keith and I hid around the corner.

One by one the latecomers arrived to pick up a copy of the paper, ritually deposit their token piece of debris, then depart at high speed. Keith or I would nip to the front door and the three ladies, armed with a torch, would whisper the details of the aforesaid debris through the letterbox before collapsing with laughter. We would then chase the culprit, ask him why he had deposited only an old French franc and two bent nails and demand the full fivepence.

The fun of the game lay in the victim's wriggling. Most of those we caught, looking back in desperation at the darkened, locked shop front, hadn't the faintest idea how we'd uncovered them — yet such was the accuracy of our information that eventually, after much squirming, they would admit their crime and much to our delight would scurry away into the night.

*The long arm of the Press.*

The game came to an abrupt end one night when we caught an acting Chief Inspector of Police at it. The thought of 20 years worth of carefully cultivated contacts drying up at a stroke sent Keith into a nervous tremor and we never played it again.

This was a pity because on the winter evenings there wasn't much to keep me occupied. I had been living in a tiny flat directly above the office and, after frequent forays to the local pub which blew all my cash at the beginning of the week, there was little to do but read and keep falling in love.

I read a book about Richard Dimbleby, and once again my thoughts turned to broadcasting. Dimbleby had started his journalistic career on the same paper I now worked for. He had lived in exactly the same place and covered exactly the same area as I now did and he, too, had found the New Forest a lonely place for strangers. The boldness with which Dimbleby had eventually approached the BBC had made a great impression.

One night I brought the love-of-my-life back to the flat and she stayed the night. The next morning, my day off, we heard the three cheerful ladies arrive as usual for work down below.

Undeterred by our ancient bed, which creaked badly, we stayed where we were — all morning.

In the afternoon after my girlfriend had slipped quietly away, I stuck my head round the shop to see that everthing was all right.

'Afternoon ladies!' I chirped.

'Afternoon, Nigel!' came back the chorus, accompanied by a barrage of huge grins.

I detected something slightly wrong.

'Everything OK, ladies?' I asked.

'Everything's fine, thank you Nigel,' came back the reply, again in unison.

Still they all stared at me, grins reaching from ear to ear.

Eventually one of them said: 'Had a nice sleep-in this morning, Nigel?'

I felt myself redden slightly.

'Yes, thanks.'

'You really must do something about mending that bed of yours.'

A huge, lascivious wink followed.

That did it.

Amidst the laughter I stood there like a stuffed lemon blushing until the roots of my hair were tingling.

That really did it. It was time to move on again.

I knew Keith knew that they knew, and he knew I knew it, but being a decent sort of a fellow he didn't mention it, although he went around the place unable to disguise a slight smirk on his face.

That really did it.

About a week later Keith got a tip that a big police search was underway on the cliff-tops for a senile old man who had been found missing from a local county council home. The cliff face was continually crumbling into the sea and the area had become very dangerous. The police had set up a mobile unit to coordinate hundreds of officers brought in from all over the New Forest. Tracker dogs were being used and a Royal Navy helicopter had been brought in to skim the cliff-tops in the search for clues to the man's disappearance.

*The lure of broadcasting.*

It was a good local story that normally Keith would have covered but he was busy so I went down to do what I could. It was an exciting scene, with rows of policemen with sticks and dogs straining at the leash sweeping across the windswept moorland to the cliff edge and the long lines of white-topped waves of the Solent beyond.

I parked beside a radio car that had been sent down to cover the story from the BBC local radio station in Southampton. The huge aerial that stretched up from the roof of the car was bending in the wind and the reporter, armed with earphones and holding a microphone, was standing just by the door, leaning forward to prevent himself being blown over.

I looked at my watch. It was exactly 11 o'clock. I climbed back into the car and turned on the radio. Suddenly the story of the lost man was introduced by a newsreader in the studio, and the station went over to a live report from the radio car just a few yards away from where I was sitting.

I could see the reporter's lips moving and his words, swept by the sea wind, chattered excitedly throught the radio loudspeaker. It was a strange, thrilling feeling, sitting on the cliff-top, watching the reporter, and listening.

Just then the naval helicopter swooped low over us and the sound of its throbbing rotor-blades was picked up by the microphone and made the radio loudspeaker vibrate. It all sounded so much more urgent, so much more real then ever my printed story could.

I went back to the office, typed out a dozen paragraphs for the late editions, 'phoned them over, then wrote a long letter to the BBC in Southampton.

It wasn't as eloquent as Richard Dimbleby's but it was the best I could do.

# 4

It was 3.30 a.m.

Inside my head a pair of bells was ringing agonisingly. Like a burglar alarm, there was no one about who could turn them off. Mercilessly, they rattled against the bones of my skull.

As I opened my eyes in the darkness, a headache began pounding away like a lunatic with a sledgehammer. Then I realised the telephone was ringing. I struggled, naked, out of bed, and fell flat on my face. I had been asleep for no more than an hour and a half after a long evening drinking malt whisky with an old Scottish friend. Friend! I cursed him now, the whisky still swilling around my cold and heaving stomach, as I crawled like a dying man to the telephone.

The voice at the other end of the line made my mind spin still further.

It belonged to Steve, the news editor at the local radio station where I had just started work.

Steve had a strange sense of humour.

'Got a hangover?' enquired the voice, in its rough Lincolnshire accent.

I grunted, animal-like, and the voice tut-tutted irritatingly.

'Been a naughty boy again? Naughty, naughty, naughty!'

So far, I think you will agree, the conversation lacked any great dramatic or literary quality. Worse still, it seemed to me, was that it lacked any point. Was Steve ringing up just for a chat? At 3.30 a.m.?

'Is this a social call, Steve?' I managed to croak.

'Far from it, dear boy.' He paused. 'I want you to come to work — now.'

I looked at my watch again. 3.30 a.m. exactly. Was he joking?

'Work? Now?'

'And get moving. There's been an IRA bomb attack here in Southampton. There may be more to come. Move fast.'

With that the line went dead.

I felt sick throughout the half-hour drive to Southampton. Last night's meal — a quiche with acres of mushroom and red pepper, I suddenly remembered with nauseating clarity — was joining forces with large quantities of white wine and the malt whisky and was threatening to leave my stomach at any moment to make an imminent return to the outside world.

I managed to stave off disaster only because I was distracted by the huge numbers of policemen lining the streets of the centre of the city. Whole areas had been completely sealed off. Some blocks of shops were glistening in the darkness beneath rows of piercing floodlights. In the shadows there were troops, some on guard, some prowling, on patrol. Occasionally I passed a line of civilians, dressed in a hurry, with tousled hair and pale, frightened faces, evacuated from their homes. The city seemed to be shrouded in an eerie, expectant silence. It was like a war, and in one sense of course it was.

I had stopped at a road block and after identifying myself I was escorted to the Central Police Station. Our radio car had already been parked outside by one of the radio station's engineers. He gave me a quick, worried smile as I went inside.

Fighting back the growing waves of nausea which had started to reappear, I was shown into a large briefing room where half a dozen reporters and photographers were already sitting in silence.

After a few minutes the door suddenly opened and in marched a Detective Chief Superintendant, flanked by two senior CID men.

The policeman looked tired and haggard. At length he lifted his head wearily, and spoke to us in slow, solemn tones. 'Gentlemen, there was a most serious incident in the centre of Southampton tonight. One bomb has already exploded in the shopping precinct, wrecking a shop and damaging others nearby, and we have discovered what we believe to be a second bomb, as yet unexploded. We fear there may be other bombs. I hardly need remind you of the seriousness of the situation.'

He paused, ominously, for the weight of his words to sink in.

'Gentlemen, are there any questions?'

I put up my hand immediately. I was desperate.

'Where is the nearest gents, please?'

I ran down the corridor like a bat out of hell and just made it in time. All the gelignite in the world could have gone off at that moment for all I cared.

After a few minutes I staggered out of the police station to the radio car and called up the Operations Room back at the radio station a few miles away.

It was no good saying I was about to die. Steve was on the other end.

'London want you to do a live inject into the national radio news in five minutes time — they want a thirty-second report, O.K. dear boy?'

I nodded. They couldn't see that of course but words were beyond me.

I scribbled some words on the back of an old cigarette packet summarising the few facts I had been able to absorb and a few minutes later, after a deep breath of fresh air, I was broadcasting to the nation. As I finished with the usual phrase '. . . and now back to the studio' my poor stomach gave another heave of volcanic proportions, much to the amusement of a large police sergeant standing nearby.

If only the nation had known.

• • •

The radio station was much smaller than I had expected. Although it broadcast to an area with a population of over a million, the staff consisted of no more than 30 producers, presenters, engineers, journalists and secretaries. It sat on the third floor of an old converted hotel near the run-down dockland area of the city, although the building still vibrated from time to time as the London train rumbled past the door bearing its cargo of old and wealthy travellers, en route to the port's Ocean Terminal and the luxury liners which still plied the profitable routes to South Africa and North America.

At one end of the station there was a main transmission studio, Studio One, and two smaller recording studios. This was linked by a long, winding hotel corridor to a disc and tape library, and a few administrative and production offices. At the other end there was a large newsroom. Steve's kingdom. Steve was a broad, powerfully-built young man with a fearsome black beard and a legendary reputation in his home county of Lincolnshire for his capacity for beer. Work, like play, was pursued with great vigour; his standards were high, and so was the confidence to tell his staff when their standards weren't high enough.

The local news bulletins lasted either five or ten minutes. They were compiled, written and read by one of Steve's four harassed news producers, and consisted of stories 'phoned in by local newspaper correspondents or gathered from calls we regularly made to the police, and the other emergency services. There would also be news picked up from local councils, the docks or from industry, from the newspapers themselves, or even from members of the public direct.

The producer would only have one, or at the most, two reporters working for him. Together they would assemble two or three interviews to illustrate their bulletin, recorded on location or over the telephone.

It was very hard work. Throughout the day the bulletins were updated and then rewritten; updated and rewritten; and all under the hawk-like gaze of Steve, criticising, praising, questioning, cajoling. At lunchtime we would adjourn to the BBC Club Bar, where food was scarce but beer more plentiful. Then, whilst battling to maintain a steady focus and a fluent tongue, it was update, rewrite, until my head was spinning and my ears were burning from telephone call after telephone call.

Unlike the BBC's national network radio, where each live programme comes from a different studio, all the station's output had to come from Studio One. The place usually ended up looking like Piccadilly Circus.

A few minutes before the news, the producer and his reporter, armed with their scripts, would hurry down the long corridor and creep into Studio One like a couple of burglars whilst the DJ sitting beside his bank of turntables wound up his show. This presented in-built hazards. Chairs were knocked over, records dropped, coffee spilt amid barrages of 'sssssh!' After lunch the disruption was usually greater than before, and the 'sssssh!' replaced by a hissed: 'Shut yer bleedin cakehole!' or similar niceties.

Once the news team had successfully negotiated a path across the studio, they sat down at a large round table in the corner of the studio with a huge black microphone in the middle that looked old enough to have been used in some of Churchill's famous wartime broadcasts. Then, with the bulletin successfully under way, it was the turn of the DJ to tiptoe out, silently waving a goodbye or an obscene gesture, depending how his show had gone.

The longer or more important stories were split so that a short introduction was read by the producer and the details were then given in a live report or 'voice-piece' from the reporter. On my third day at work, Steve himself was reading the news and I sat opposite him sweatily fingering a long and complicated voice-piece he had written for me.

Steve believed in baptism by fire.

My first instinct was to self-destruct by shouting something terribly rude. Somehow that aged microphone held some mysterious power over me, the fact that it was live taunting me to bellow 'Bum!' or 'Balls!' Beyond the large, soundproofed glass window I watched a solitary engineer pottering about the Operations Room silently whistling a tune to himself and casually playing-in our taped

*Remembering grandmother's advice on radio reporting.*

interviews as required. A red light glowed by the door; on the wall a silent clock measured the passing seconds. It all seemed a little unreal; gratefully I remembered my grandmother's words of advice: 'Just try to imagine you are addressing a room full of cauliflowers, dear, and you'll be just fine.'

Suddenly Steve was saying: '. . . and this report from Nigel Farrell' and, resisting the urge to launch into a tirade of four-letter words, I was away.

When it was over I couldn't remember whether I had done well or badly. In a daze I stood up, turned round, walked straight into my chair and with a mighty crash that reverberated around the studio, I fell flat on the floor.

I started work at the same time as another young reporter, Ian, who was so full of nervous energy that his long, thin body topped with an explosion of wild, curly blond hair seemed to twitch and wriggle as though a continuous electrical current was passing through him.

At that time Southampton had a thriving IRA cell and the city was constantly in the news for shootings or the discovery of explosives. On his first day Ian had been nervously sitting in the newsroom looking helpful when a call came through to the duty news producer. It was a tip-off that a large quantity of gelignite had been discovered at a block of flats in Southampton called Albion Towers. Ian was tossed one of the station's small, portable German Uher tape recorders which he had never even seen before and told to get his ass down there pronto.

Despite getting lost several times, Ian found the block and wandered innocently into it just as the police cordoned off the entire area. It turned out that the gelignite was part of a big haul of IRA explosives hidden in a garage that was intended to blow-up the liner QE2. As word got about the crowds formed outside and the first of teams of news camera crews and photographers began to arrive. Lines of policemen were instructed to keep everyone well away.

Ian, without realising it, was the only journalist inside the building. He gathered a few facts by talking to a pair of detectives (who assumed he'd been allowed through the cordon by some special dispensation) and then, quite by accident, stumbled across the only eye-witness to have actually observed the IRA men coming

61

and going with their explosives. After thinking about it for a while, Ian thought perhaps he'd better interview the man just in case.

'I don't suppose you have any idea how this tape recorder works?' he asked politely, and the man said he thought he did, and together they tried each button and switch until they had mastered the machine and Ian could record an interview. He then interviewed the garage owner, a next-door neighbour and even a senior police officer before beetling back to the studio.

When Ian told his producer, with some apprehension, what he had done, the fellow's eyes positively bulged with surprise and admiration. 'You're a bloody genius!' he said.

Like all the BBC's local radio stations, Southampton has a direct radio link with London and within the hour Ian's exclusive coverage of the week's biggest news story was being broadcast on Radio 4's 'The World This Weekend' and on national radio and television bulletins throughout the day. Afterwards the Duty News Editor in London rang Ian and thanked him for his professional expertise.

'How long have you been in the job?' he asked Ian.

'Oh about six hours,' came the reply.

Of course Ian became something of a legend for his reporting prowess, and he soon became known for his intrepid style. He was thrown down the gangplank of a ship which had been taken over by striking seamen, and was mauled by Secret Service men when he got an exclusive interview with President Carter's son Chip on a visit to Britain. But despite all the physical twitching and wriggling he never worried about a thing. Over the next few months he and I learnt the business together. He turned out to be a much more dedicated operator than ever I was; as far as we could gather, he lived in his old battered Ford, equipped with primus stove and sleeping bag, so that he could always be on hand for a story. He was very secretive about his private life and used to take his holidays in Moscow.

One morning, a few days after the dazzling success with the IRA cache, Ian was asked to produce the news bulletins, a doubtful privilege because he was allocated me, equally green, as his reporter. Together we muddled though the morning. Once again I was given a live voice piece and together we walked nervously down the long corridor to Studio One for the lunchtime bulletin. We managed to manoeuvre ourselves successfully to the newsdesk without so much as a whisper or cough and I was gripping a copy of my story in my cold, clammy hand and apprehensively reading it through for the thousandth time when I suddenly received a sharp kick in the shins. Biting back the pain, I looked up at Ian on the other side of the table; his face was undergoing a rapid series of curious contortions. He had turned very pale and the twitching and wriggling had achieved spasmodic proportions.

At first I thought he was having a coronary; then, as I looked on, horrified, he suddenly began to scribble a message on a piece of paper which he then thrust towards me.

The message, in violent, panic-stricken hand, said: 'I've brought *yesterday's* lunchtime bulletin.'

Now this was serious. The DJ on the other side of the studio was saying farewell to his listeners, his signature music was already on air, the clock read exactly 1 p.m. and the newsroom was a long way away.

I looked again at Ian. He gazed back in frozen agony; unless I moved, and fast, he would have no choice but to read yesterday's news. Steve would go berserk.

I tiptoed out of the studio, like a man on hot bricks, and ran demented all the way back to the newsroom. There was the bulletin, today's bulletin, lying in a neat pile on Ian's desk. I grabbed it and like a bullet from a gun shot back down the corridor and into the studio, where the DJ was frantically filling in time by repeating the station's frequency, over and over again.

I flung the bulletin at Ian and, with the crisis apparently over, we were into the news and I was slumped over the table attempting to regain my breath without making any sound whatever.

Try it sometime. Not easy.

With my pulse racing, my lungs wouldn't work fast enough; as Ian ploughed into the bulletin, I gulped down lungfulls of air, whilst fighting to suppress a rattly asthmatic wheeze which had suddenly appeared.

Then, quite out of the blue, I heard Ian introduce my voice piece. Of course I had assumed that after my obvious ordeal and acute shortage of breath he would simply read it himself; but not, there it was, '. . . for more details, here is Nigel Farrell. . .'

For a moment I could only look at him in astonishment, and he could only look back at me in desperation as the bastard slowly realised what he had done.

A long pause filled the airwaves.

I had no choice. With my lungs at bursting-point, I grimly stared down at my mangled piece of script and began to read.

Afterwards friends told me I had sounded like a dying man.

I managed to get out only one or two words at a time. In the long pauses between speech I desperately sucked in more air, forgetting at the same time to breathe out. Gradually, as that first sentence was dragged out syllable by syllable, my chest began to inflate like a hot-air balloon. I managed to continue for a few more moments until a number of beautifully coloured stars suddenly started whizzing across my sight, turning and twisting magnificently like astral Catherine wheels in a frosty night sky.

Then everything went black.

I only passed out for a split second but, by the grace of God, Ian had managed to pull himself together, plunge in and take over the rest of my script.

Afterwards the only words of consolation Ian offered were: 'Christ, sorry mate,' which I didn't consider quite adequate. I resolved to pay him back.

Later Steve showed me a little metal box that always sat beside the microphone on which there was a small white plastic switch called a cough button. When this was pressed, the microphone went dead, allowing the user to cough/splutter/vomit/die unbeknown to the listening audience.

'My advice, dear boy, is to treat it with some respect,' Steve said, and told me a story about a former colleague whose career had come to a premature end because the cough button hadn't been working properly. The poor fellow had become so bored with news reading that very late one night, in order to amuse the sound engineer, he had pressed the button at the end of each phrase so the news went something like this:

Today the President of France, Monsieur Pompidou, announced a new package of economic measures.

*Pause. Cough button depressed.*

. . . silly old fart . . .

*Cough Button off*
The move is designed to strengthen the value of the Franc . . .
*Pause*
. . .big deal!. . . .
*Pause*
. . .as well as boost industrial investment.
*Pause*
. . .what a whopper!
etc., etc.

This did indeed amuse the sound engineer but unfortunately the cough button was broken and every word was transmitted.

For the first time in my life I was working hard. In the past, long periods of tedium had been broken up by the occasional burst of enthusiasm; now I found I had to be constantly searching for stories and ideas or I was in trouble. We were a small team and, unlike the world of newspapers, here you were enthusiastic and consistently so because there was no spare capacity.

Everyone was pushed a little harder by Steve. Three or four times a day he would burst from his little office at the end of the newsroom frantically waving pieces of paper in the air and shouting: 'Great idea, dear boy, great idea!' and then ask you to do an interview with a freefall parachutist in situ or record your impressions of being hugged by a gorilla.

On one occasion Steve asked me to get an interview with John Cordle, the former MP for Bournemouth East who had resigned his seat in Parliament because of his connections with the jailed architect John Poulson. Cordle wasn't talking to anyone, but nevertheless Steve suggested I wait outside his house for at least 24 hours just in case and so that's exactly what I did.

Steve had been an outstanding reporter in his own right and this motivated us all, too, in order to stop the wretched fellow saying: 'Of course, dear boy, if I'd been handling this interview . . . ' or 'When I was a reporter we always used to . . . '

Steve had made his name in Nottingham where he worked on the notorious Black Panther story: the Panther, you may remember, was a former SAS man who kidnapped a young girl and kept her hidden in a disused mineshaft before hanging her.

His capture came about by sheer luck. The Panther, so called because of the ghoulish pictures of himself he had sent to taunt the police, was walking along a street late one night when he was stopped by two constables in a patrol car. Quite routinely, they asked him who he was and where he was going at that time of night. Instead of keeping calm and trying to bluff his way out, the fugitive produced a sawn-off shotgun from his holdall and threatened to blow the policemen to pieces unless they did exactly as they were told.

He climbed into the back of the patrol car and with the gun wedged into the shoulder blade of one of the constables, they drove out of town. After a few miles the road forked; the Panther told the driver to keep left, but the policeman, pretending to make a mistake, began to turn left and then suddenly swerved to the right. Everyone was thrown off balance. In the struggle that followed, the shotgun went off, one policeman jumped out, the other began to fight the Panther, a trained SAS killer. Events would probably have come to a sticky end but for a number of Nottinghamshire miners in a fish and chip shop a few yards from where the car finally screeched to a halt. Hearing the shouting the miners charged over to the stricken policemen like a detachment of US Cavalry and, after one of the most famous enquiries in police history, the Black Panther was caged at last.

Steve had covered much of the court case for local radio. After the Panther had finally been convicted, Steve engineered a superb little exclusive. He waited for all the reporters to pack up and go home and then managed to persuade the two constables to re-live their awful ordeal. With Steve sitting on the back seat with a tape-recorder perched on his knee, they drove the same patrol car down that same Nottinghamshire street, stopped at the same place, drove on to the same fork in the road and then to the scene of the fight. As they drove, Steve noticed in the rear-view mirror that both men were sweating profusely; words tumbled out of them as they described with piercing clarity what had happened, almost as if they were relieving themselves of some great burden.

Much of a reporter's life involves persuading people to re-live their experiences; it's that extra piece of imagination needed to get to the kernel of the experience which makes the difference between a good reporter and an average one.

Under Steve's direction, too, we quickly learnt to understand news priorities ... often the hard way. One quiet morning I was sitting in the newsroom drinking mugfulls of coffee and telling Ian that joke about the one-legged Irishman locked in a brothel with a Spanish-speaking parrot when a call came through from a nearby police station. A baby had been snatched from its pram outside a shop. Could we help?

I took the details and promised to get the story on our next bulletin in an hour's time.

I finished the joke, you know, the bit where the parrot leans over the pimp and says Buena Sera, Senor, and everyone in the room fell about laughing. Then Steve burst in waving his arms about like a lunatic, no doubt with some Machiavellian story for me to cover in mind, and seeing everyone laughing I was made to repeat the joke. He didn't understand it.

Then we all settled down to do some work and Steve asked Ian if there was much news about. Ian went through his list of stories and, almost as an afterthought, mentioned the kidnapped baby.

'Has that been out on the air yet?' Steve immediately demanded.

'The next bulletin's not until eleven.'

Steve was furious. 'Damn the next bulletin. Go down to the studio *now* and get that information out in a newsflash.'

When Ian returned, he was packed off in the radio car for live broadcasts from the scene of the snatch and I was kicked out and told to report from the police station with the latest developments every fifteen minutes. Steve tossed out the entire morning's programme schedules and instead listeners were kept informed, minute by minute, of the hunt for the kidnapper and invited to phone the police with any clues.

As a result, the baby, and the man who took it from its pram, had been tracked down by detectives before lunchtime.

● ● ●

This was a time for mastering the ground rules of broadcasting. I got an exclusive interview with Lord Carrington but forgot to turn on the tape-recorder; I covered a major political speech by Michael Foot but unfortunately I used a tape-spool that I had been sitting on in the car and the poor man sounded as though he had swallowed a box of tennis balls. I had doors slammed in my face, my microphone snatched away, and twice put myself on air without realising it.

Technical disasters appeared in my path like elephant traps.

I arrived for work one morning and was told to take the radio car for some live interviews with striking Ford workers on duty outside a local car plant. This filled me with dread. The radio car had a huge, retractable aerial with a compressed air mechanism to make it go up and down. This I did not understand.

When I arrived at the gates of the plant I was cordially greeted by a barrage of jeers and wolf-whistles. A few days before one of the unions involved had accused the radio station of bias and the arrival of a young, nervous-looking reporter in a flashy radio car was not well received.

I parked the car and began my doomed attempt to get the aerial up. Several short, meaningful references were made to my parentage and to my sexual inclinations. I talked to the office on the radio-telephone link and Steve told me he wanted my interviews in five minutes. As I was talking, the pickets closed in around the car in an angry mob.

I had a feeling that they might derive a certain degree of satisfaction from tearing me limb from limb so instead of getting out again I gingerly wound down the window and said:

'I say, you chaps, anyone fancy being interviewed?'

This led to more suggestions about what could be done to my vitals, and bags more hostile cheering. The radio/telephone burst into life again: 'Three minutes to go, Nigel — and we're still not receiving your transmissions. Is your aerial fully extended?'

In desperation and near panic I suddenly jumped out of the car and shouted: 'Damn your stupid strike, does anyone here know how to work this bloody aerial?'

There was a short, stunned silence. Then one man stepped forward. 'What's the problem, cocker?'

I explained and he said: 'If I was to get a plank, cocker, and wedge the end of it beneath the tip of the aerial I could push the thing up ten or twelve feet. Any good?'

He tramped off and in seconds was back with a vast piece of timber and was pushing up the aerial.

*Desperate measures.*

I tried the microphone; the office said the reception had improved but was still not good enough for broadcast.

Another picket came forward. ' 'Ere, Teddy if you was to sit on my shoulders and hold the plank we might get the soddin' thing high enough.'

'Gotcha, Mervin.'

Better, said the office, but still too much interference.

Only two minutes to go before on air.

By now, it seemed the entire Ford work force was involved in overcoming the problem.

All over the yard groups of men were standing about scratching their heads and discussing what best to do.

Suddenly, a van appeared and was backed up alongside the radiocar. I watched in amazement as Mervin clambered up onto its roof, Teddy scrambled up and balanced on his shoulders and then pushed up the aerial with the plank.

Perfect, said the office.

Within 30 seconds I was on air, and the pickets were fighting amongst themselves to be interviewed.

Steve had a wry smile on his face when I finally got back to base.

'Well done, dear boy, well done. I don't know why but I had imagined you might have been in for a hostile reception down there. Any trouble with the pickets?'

I looked at him, puzzled.

'Couldn't have been more helpful, Steve.'

# 5

It promised to be a spectacular occasion.

For the first time in nearly a quarter of century, the ships of the Royal Navy would be gathered together in one place — off Spithead — for the Queen's Review of the Fleet. In all, nearly 180 ships were to be inspected by the Royal Family on board the Royal Yacht *Britannia*, which would weave her way ceremonially down the rows of big aircarft carriers, like the old *Ark Royal*, destroyers, submarines and support ships, each dressed overall with bunting, each with their crews lining the decks like cheering, happy matchstick-men.

The day before the Review proper the liner *QE2* was to sail from Southampton on one of her regular transatlantic trips. Cunard's public relations department, never one to miss an opportunity, decided the ship should set sail via Spithead and through the lines of naval vessels awaiting Review; the image of the world's greatest passenger liner slowly passing some of the most famous military ships of the day with waving passengers, accompanied by the sound of foghorns booming, would be a powerful one. It was perfectly stage-managed; Cunard even laid on a sparkling summer sun which made the gentle waters of the Solent shimmer with light and the ships glisten in the brightness.

Armed with a tape-recorder, I was told to be aboard the *QE2* and arrange 'vox-pops' interviews with the mostly American passengers, who would be expected to describe in admiring terms the scene spread before them.

This was an easy task; once I had recorded the vox-pops and a short voice report, I would be free to take advantage of the facilities of the *QE2* for the time it took the liner to reach her first port of call on the other side of the Channel, at Cherbourg. There, most of the assembled TV crews, photographers and reporters would disembark and be flown home in an aeroplane specially chartered by Cunard.

All went swimmingly. I recorded my materail quickly and repaired at once to the biggest bar on board where I joined cohorts of other pressmen already well stuck in to the gallons of gin and tonic being provided by a helpful PR man. I settled back comfortably in an armchair and prepared to enjoy myself.

After a forgettable number of G and Ts had been consumed and life was just beginning to seem distinctly rosy, a Cunard officer appeared at our table and asked if there was anyone present by the name of Farrell.

I owned up, and we all giggled idiotically.

'We've just had a call from your office on the radio telephone,' he said sternly.

'And how are they today?' I asked, happy in the knowledge that at last I was safely beyond the reach of any of Steve's loony ideas.

'They want you to get off the ship immediately.'

Even in my euphoric state, this statement sounded rather alarming.

'Get off?'

'Get off.'

'Get off now?'

'Get off now.'

This exchange would have continued indefinitely had not the officer held up his hand for silence and explained.

'Apparently they want you back in the office for another story. They've asked that you should be taken off the ship when the pilot cutter arrives to pick up the pilot. I'm afraid this involves climbing down the side of the ship on a rope-ladder — obviously we can't afford to stop the ship just for the pilot so we'll still be going forward at some speed.'

'A rope ladder?'

'A rope ladder, sir.'

'And you don't even slow down?'

'No, sir. The pilot cutter will draw alongside at the same speed as the ship and you have to jump.'

This was appalling. The reader may have gathered by now that this honest and hard-working reporter is not the bravest man ever to have lived and frankly the prospect of climbing down the side of one of the world's biggest liners and leaping onto a little boat bobbing alongside at high speed did not fill me with great enthusiasm.

Fortunately, the effects of all those G and Ts helped soften the experience; but even now, in the cold, dark and lonely hours of the very early morning I sometimes awake in a cold sweat and once more see the huge side of that giant ship towering above me and once more feel that incessant tingling in my vital organs — an affliction which regularly appears at moments of great jeopardy.

*A change of assignment.*

Somehow I survived the jump — like torture-victims the actual, painful moment of lift-off has been erased from my memory — and when I staggered back into the office Steve sent me out to interview the chairman of a parish council protesting about a 2p increase in car park charges.

'You didn't really believe, dear boy, that I was actually going to pay you to get plastered in total luxury all the way to France, now did you?' he asked, grinning, and I said no I hadn't really believed that at all.

Nightmares about the *QE2* weren't the only dreams that had begun to plague my mind. Broadcasting live, day after day, had started to play funny little tricks inside my head. With experience I had managed to go beyond the 'bum and balls syndrome' of dreaming about shouting obscenities into the live microphone, but now both Ian and I found it had been replaced by another, very real fear — giggling.

The most ridiculous trivialities would set us off. In the middle of one news bulletin I would drop a spider onto Ian's script and in the middle of the next he would produce a clothes peg whilst I was reading a voice-piece and push it on my nose. The nearest we ever got to total breakdown was when Ian stumbled over the words 'Prime Minister Jim Callaghan' in a bulletin. For some reason best known to himself, Ian decided spontaneously that he should insert 'Mr' in front of every man's name in the remainder of the script so that when he came to my voice-piece he announced: 'This report now from *Mister* Nigel Farrell . . . ' which sounded quite absurd.

As I started to read my script, I noticed out of the corner of my eye that Ian was stuffing a handkerchief in his mouth, an action synchronised with a regular heaving up and down of the shoulders. It was only as I was drawing to a close that I realised the poor fellow was convulsed with laughter.

By luck I had a complete copy of the script in front of me so I read on, my own voice now trembling and wavering on the verge of breaking down, until Ian had recovered sufficiently to take over.

A very close shave indeed.

Ian arrived very late for work one morning and I noticed his wriggling about was worse than ever. He looked pale and wan after a fitful night's sleep in the back of the Ford.

'I had this fearful dream, time and time again,' he told me in a feverish whisper. 'I was reading a bulletin and as I read I realised that the second half of each sentence was missing. I had to ad-lib all the blank spaces in the script.' He shuffled off down the corridor wearily shaking his head like an old man.

That night I had the same dream.

In Moscow, the Politbureau has announced that . . .
At home, the Employment Secretary says the annual rate of inflation has increased again because . . .
Now cricket, and at Lord's England are . . .

It was quite horrible, not at all amusing, and I made up my mind

74

that if anything like it ever really happened the best policy was simply to tell the truth and at least let the listeners enjoy a joke.

Another aspect of the job which we had to learn to cope with was looking daft whilst we were broadcasting in public — a useful preparation for the crazy world of television that lay ahead.

A few weeks after the disastrous *QE2* episode Steve sent me to Chichester to cover an official visit by the Queen to the Royal Military Police barracks just outside the city. Security was strict; the Queen was to arrive by Royal Train at Chichester station and be driven by Rolls-Royce to the barracks. Three official black limousines were being provided for the press corps and because of the security problem it was made quite clear that journalists *must* remain with the press party at all times.

'The Queen is due to arrive at the station at 11 o'clock sharp, so do us a live telephone report into the news then, and afterwards prepare a short recorded package about the rest of the visit for the lunchtime news.' said Steve, making it sound straight-forward.

As always in these things, the theory and the practice were miles apart. The Queen arrived spot on schedule and the telephone bit went splendidly, with me at pains to point out that the Queen was wearing an elegant orange knee-length chiffon coat with matching hat ('We'll lost 100,000 female listeners if you forget to mention her dress, dear boy').

I emerged from the telephone box, however, just in time to see the Royal Rolls speed off down the road at high-speed followed by the three press limousines and half-a-dozen army motorcycle escorts. I tried desperately to run after the convoy but I was stopped by a large policeman who asked me for proof of identity.

'You've rather missed the boat on this one, lad,' he said sympathetically when I explained. 'You'll never catch up with that lot, and even if you do they won't let you into the barracks.'

'But what about my press pass?'

The policeman slowly shook his head. 'Not with things being as they are, lad. You've missed the boat all right.'

As the crowds dispersed from the station, I began to mooch about miserably wondering how to salvage things. The vision of a furious Steve provided a useful stimulus. Saying it wasn't my fault wouldn't be enough.

I walked aimlessly into a park, sat down on a bench and studied what material I had about the visit. As usual, the Central Office of Information, the body which often organises such bunfights, had sent us reams of bumph about the Queen's schedule. Typically every minute of the day had been meticulously planned, the names and ranks of those involved listed in exact order of introduction, a short history of the building provided etc., etc.

I decided the only course of action was to write and record a short report there and then, in the park, and after scribbling wildly for ten minutes I stood up, turned on the tape recorder, and holding the microphone the regulation one foot away from my face I cleared my throat and began:

> There's a great feeling of excitement and apprehension here in the chilly wintry sunshine at the Royal Military Police barracks. And here comes the Queen now, waving to the crowds of servicemen's families who have waited so patiently to greet her, and being borne in one of the regiment's green open-backed Landrovers. And as the Landrover draws to a halt, the Queen is met by the Commandant, a Lieutenant-Major who until last year was serving in Northern Ireland ... and she's now being handed a charming bouquet of flowers by the Commandant's daughter, nine year old Clare Elizabeth ...

You get the idea. Anyway I completed what I decided was a superb improvised eye-witness report and was just turning off the tape machine when I realised I was being rather oddly stared at by an old man carrying some shopping, a freckly-faced boy with a bleeding left knee and a three-legged poodle.

I smiled at them reassuringly. The old man hobbled over and said: ''Ere, mate, what you up to then, eh?'

'It's quite all right, don't be alarmed,' I said, 'I work for the BBC.'

As I was to discover so often in other cases, this explanation usually provided a perfectly acceptable excuse for the most lunatic behaviour and, his curiosity apparently satisfied, the old man gave a knowing nod and hobbled off.

After my report had been broadcast I wondered how my future would have fared if the Queen had broken her leg getting out of that

*'And here comes the Queen now, waving to the crowd of servicemen's families.'*

Landrover or if she had been assassinated, but the consequences were too dire to contemplate for long.

Shortly afterwards Ian was sent out in the radio car for a live report on an overnight fire which destroyed part of a hostel for homeless people. While he was giving his report on air a woman passing by, not realising what he was doing, actually asked him if he knew the time; and Ian actually told her.

Can you imagine it?

**Ian**: Detectives believe the fire may have been deliberately started because they've found evidence that ...
**Woman**: (*Off mike*) Got the time, luv?
**Ian**: ... found evidence of petrol in the basement ...
**Woman**: (*Louder*) I said got the time? You deaf or something?
**Ian**: (*Annoyed*) What do you want?
**Woman**: The time!
**Ian**: Er ... um ... it's two minutes past nine.
**Woman**: Sorry I asked!
**Ian**: ... and forensic experts are now being called to the scene.

Much more rivetting listening than ever a smooth version would have been, I think you'll agree.

● ● ●

There was one reporter on the station from whom we all learnt a great deal; his name was Peter, and he was completely blind. His loss of sight, far from being a handicap, was a positive asset in the world of radio.

Peter thought in terms of sounds instead of pictures and his reports were some of the best I have ever heard.

One advantage he had over the rest of us was that his blindness often opened doors closed to everyone else. When sent on a difficult assignment, Peter would always take his white stick with him and wave this fiercely in the face of any opposition. When there were people to be interviewed who were all ready to slam the door in the face of any other reporter, Peter was offered cups of tea and cream cakes. When pressmen were jostling to get into an area cordoned off by the police after a murder or fire, Peter would simply march past detectives and constables alike with sweeping strokes of his white stick, as though he owned the place.

He was also a man tough enough to be able to laugh at his own disability. He would play football with his children in his garden during the afternoon and run about hopelessly whilst they scored goal after goal against him; then he'd wait until nightfall and pitch dark before taking them on again and, as they fell over each other in the darkness, he'd thrash them.

I once heard Peter give a brilliant radio commentary on a game of blind cricket. You may be surprised to know that blind cricket has become quite popular in recent years; the players use a ball which has little metal bearings rattling around inside it so that everyone can hear it bounce along the ground. Whilst it's taken very seriously there is obviously a comic element; if, for example, the batsman manages to give the ball a good whack! as it clatters down the pitch there is a real danger it will come to a silent stop somewhere in the outfield. The match then has to be suspended for all hands to locate the wretched thing.

Peter caught just the right flavour of the occasion. Afterwards some unsuspecting listeners accused him of patronising the blind. How would he like it, they asked, if he had lost his sight?

Peter did have trouble editing tape in a hurry. Normally this is a very simple affair; on playing back tape reel-to-reel, a mark is made with a chinagraph pencil on the point where an edit is to be made, the unwanted section is then cut away with a razor blade and the two loose ends rejoined with sticky tape.

One night I had to stay late in the office preparing the bulletin for early next morning. At midnight I turned my attention to an interview Peter had done earlier in the day with William Whitelaw. Although he had been asked to supply only one-and-a-half minutes, the interview ran for a full seven minutes and took a long time to edit.

I was annoyed Peter hadn't done it himself and the next day I told him so. It was only when the poor man was apologising and explaining how in the past he'd lacerated most of his fingers whilst trying to edit that I suddenly remembered that he was unable to see.

'Peter, Peter, I'm terribly sorry,' I said, holding my hands up in the air to stop him talking — a rather futile gesture under the circumstances. 'I'm so sorry, I had forgotten your blindness.'

Peter stood there without saying a word for a moment, and I began to feel slightly uncomfortable.

'Thanks, Nigel,' he said at length. 'That's the best thing you ever said to me.'

Blind or not, Steve kept driving us hard, day in, day out. Nothing seemed to daunt him from the task of getting out the best programmes possible. He was always right on our tails, knocking us into a team, pushing aside any obstacles with a dismissive flick of his hand.

One morning the newspapers were full of a story about the alleged subversive activities of the South African secret police in Britain. It was claimed that agents of the Bureau of State Security — BOSS — had been illicitly gathering information about a number of black nationalist leaders based in this country. There had been accusations that BOSS men had broken into the offices of several organisations and groups and stolen files.

Because several individuals from our part of the world were named in the articles, Steve decided there was a strong enough local angle for us to give some coverage to the story. He told me to get on with it.

I tried to contact several of the individuals involved but got nowhere. Then I rang the South African embassy in London; they didn't want to know. Even the organisations where the break-ins had apparently occurred were unhelpful — they'd 'be in contact' later.

When I told this to Steve he said: 'What do BOSS say?'

'BOSS?'

'Yes, BOSS. Have you spoken to them?'

This sounded a little unrealistic to me, and I said so.

Steve puffed his chest up and flicked the braces on his trousers several times.

'This isn't some tinpot little provincial weekly newspaper, dear boy!' he said pompously. 'This is the British Broadcasting Corporation, famed throughout the world! 'Phone 'em up!'

''Phone up BOSS?'

''Phone 'em up!'

I decided that Steve was trying to make a point — after all, do you expect to be able to ring MI5 or the KGB? And even if you *could* ring them would someone on the end of the line say 'Good morning, MI5, thank you for ringing, can I help you?'

To keep Steve happy I rang up international enquiries and wearily asked if, under 'B' in the South African directory, there was a number for the Bureau of State Security.

Much to my astonishment I was told that indeed there was such a number. Nervously, I dialled it.

Eventually a voice on the end of the line several thousand miles away said: 'Good morning, Bureau of State Security, can I help you?'

I was so surprised that it took me several moments to gather my wits together. Then I told her I was from the BBC and the details of my enquiry and before I knew quite what was happening she had put me through to none other than the head of BOSS himself — just like that.

'Good morning, can I help you?' said the head of BOSS in a polite, clipped South African accent.

Was I really talking to the chief of one of the world's most feared secret services? I asked him about the allegations from London and he began to deny them. Could I record a short interview over the telephone? Yes of course Nigel, said the head of BOSS.

I hopped across to the little sound proofed booth at the end of the newsroom where a special telephone was wired to a tape recorder and a few minutes later I had secured a real scoop. The tape was sent to London and broadcast on the network; Steve was told to pass on London's approval to the reporter involved. Bags of initiative, they said.

Not all my missions ended so successfully. A few days later Steve burst out of his office waving his arms about wildly and shouting 'Great idea! Great idea!' We all ducked under the desks but Steve had spotted me and there was no escape.

'I have a plan,' he began ominously.

The 'plan' centred around a story about how thousands of people were defrauding local bus companies by 'over-riding' their fares. It involved the loss of millions of pounds of revenue each year, and it works like this: a passenger gets onto a busy bus and buys the cheapest possible ticket, probably for the next stop, 'A'. But instead of getting off the bus at 'A' he stays on until his real destination, which could be as far away as 'Z'. The bus conductor knows the passenger has bought a ticket but because he hasn't got a photographic memory he's unlikely to recall exactly how much the passenger paid. Thus ninety per cent of the journey is free.

'This is a good local story for us, and I have decided that the best way for us to cover it is for you to try to 'over-ride' on a bus and see how far you can get,' Steve explained.

I pointed out that the BBC couldn't be seen to be breaking the law, even if it did only involve one of its junior reporters 'over-riding' but of course Steve had already thought about that.

'Travelling on a bus without a ticket is only an offence if there is an *intention* to defraud.'

'But isn't there an intention to defraud in this case?' I asked, hopefully.

'No there is not, dear boy,' Steve announced triumphantly. 'I have already sent a five pound note to our local bus company with a letter of explanation by registered post. It will arrive tomorrow morning, a few minutes *after* you have completed your attempts to 'over-ride' on an early-morning rush-hour bus. There is therefore no *intention* to defraud at all!'

I secretly cursed his cleverness, for the project left me with a heavy heart, particularly when Steve explained that he wanted me to record a running commentary of my progress on the bus into a secret microphone pinned beneath my jumper. A length of wire was to connect it with a tape recorder carried by my side in a plastic shopping bag.

Early the following morning I reluctantly joined a small army of cackling schoolchildren in the queue at the bus-stop. At first no one took any notice of me; but as soon as the bus came into sight I fumbled in the bag to turn on the tape recorder and said out loud:

> Here comes the bus around the corner now. It's drawing up to the curb and I am about to get on.

Since I was standing quite alone my fellow waiting passengers looked up suddenly at me, startled, as I spoke. The unfortunate effect of what I was doing was compounded because to be sure of a good recording I was forced to tip my head forward to be nearer the hidden microphone; this made me appear to be suffering from a severe stiff neck.

I had to talk slowly, clearly, and quite loudly.

> I am now getting onto the bus. I will sit on the upper deck. I am now climbing the staircase. This looks a nice bus. I shall sit here and look casually out of the window so I don't draw attention to myself.

This was purgatory. Everyone was staring at me as though I was a recent escapee from a lunatic asylum. Valiantly, I ploughed on.

> Here is the conductor. He looks a pleasant chap. I wonder if he will remember me later in the journey.

A woman in the seat just in front was watching me, her eyes filled with fear. In one movement she jumped up, gathering a small child protectively towards her, and scurried away to a safe seat at the back of the bus. Others followed suit.

> I have paid the conductor the minimum fare, five pence. Now I must sit it out and see what happens.

My tortuous, idiotic monologue continued throughout the journey until I had long 'over-ridden' my fare. The story seemed to work; despite my terror, the conductor never challenged me but that could have been because he was frightened to approach me.

*A suspicious character.*

Certainly, by the time I had got off, I was the only person sitting in the front half of the bus, while about forty passengers were squeezed into the seats at the back.

Steve, nevertheless, seemed quite pleased with my efforts and that evening he offered to buy me a drink in the BBC Club. Now the club bar was just outside our reception area on the third floor of the building; it was shared with the staff of the BBC regional television station which occupied the two floors below us.

Oddly, the two groups of BBC staff scarcely ever mixed, even though each evening we all stood drinking side by side. We regarded the TV people as a load of poofy exhibitionists, and they regarded us as a rabble of boring toytown radio hams.

An excellent working relationship, I'd say.

We sat down at a small table and both downed a pint. Then we downed another. And then another. Steve liked his beer.

There was a lot of noise. Beside us a one-armed bandit rattled and gasped and rattled again; from a small billiards table in the corner of the room came the incessant chink-chink of balls smashing together; and behind us a large circle of television journalists perched precariously on bar stools were getting drunk and very loud. Over them hovered a thin, grey mist of cigarette smoke, like a giant halo.

'I gather the TV boys are looking for a new reporter,' said Steve, leaning over towards me to make himself heard. 'Interested?'

'You must be joking,' I replied quickly, annoyed that Steve had even considered me ready to defect.

He shrugged and we downed another pint.

I regarded myself as a committed radio man. When it came to fast, instant news reporting, radio was miles ahead, unimpeded by television's addiction to pictures at any cost. I felt, too, that overall radio gave the listener a far more balanced, wide-reaching view of the world than ever television could supply to the viewer.

Oh no, radio was for me and, as we downed another pint, I said so.

I looked again at the circle of TV people; many of them were familiar faces, faces we all saw every night of the week. Yet, because of the magic of television, in reality they looked superhuman, as though enclosed in a god-like aura.

We had another drink, swore eternal allegiance to radio, and forgot all about it.

About a week later, in an unusually quiet moment at work, I was browsing through the announcements on the station notice board when the advertisement for the TV reporter's job suddenly caught my eye. Somebody had scribbled over the top of it: 'Today final day for applications'.

Within an hour my application form had been completed.

•　•　•

Saying goodbye to the secure little world I had created was rather sad. Steve and Ian and a handful of the others took me out for a farewell drink but I'm afraid that under Steve's influence I embarrassed everyone by falling into a deep reverie on the gentleman's lavatory.

The next morning I arrived for my final day at work. Steve told me I was the scruffiest person he had ever worked with and suggested I should now invest in a suit for the first time in my life. Then I was handed a card signed by everyone on the station. In one corner the card was dotted with a series of little indentations: Peter had written 'good luck' on his braille typewriter.

# 6

Television is such a strange and whimsical world that in future I suggest all newcomers to the business should be gently eased into it over a period of years to allow for painless readjustment.

I was dropped straight into it from a great height and for several months verged on paranoia. Then I decided that the best chance of survival lay in jettisoning most of what I knew about journalism and beginning all over again.

The first lesson to grasp is that television is most interested not in real life but what things *look* like.

One evening, towards the end of my first week in the new job, I was baby-sitting for a friend and, with a screaming child on my lap, nearly brought disaster, quite literally, on my own head.

Whatever I tried to placate the child it bellowed on regardless and, in desperation, I picked out from its huge mountain of half-demolished playthings a new toy which I had never seen before. It was designed for very small babies and consisted of a big, transparent plastic ball with half-a-dozen smaller, coloured balls rattling around inside it. A thin plastic stem connected this to a large rubber suction pad with which the contraption could be stuck to a wall or door and bashed about endlessly by the baby.

I waggled this in front of the screaming child to no effect, but when I then plopped the thing onto my forehead so that it stuck out rather like the gun of a Dalek, the hollering suddenly stopped. Nodding my head violently up and down, the coloured balls rattled about obligingly and the child dutifully smiled, then chuckled.

All was at peace with the world.

However, having put the contented child back to bed, I ran into trouble attempting to remove the toy from my forehead. The suction pad gripped my skin so powerfully that I simply couldn't pull it off. I tried rubbing water onto it, and even soap; I pushed it and pulled it and hit it and shook it but nothing, it seemed, could break the bond 'twixt forehead and sucker.

I looked at myself in the mirror and at first found it rather amusing. It looked as though I would have to get used to the wretched thing as a permanent appendage. Ha-ha-ha!

Then a terrifying image passed through my mind. What if I really couldn't remove it? How could I read the news on television or interview the Prime Minister with a huge plastic phallus sticking out of my head like some weird gadget from outer space?

*The face of the new TV reporter has changed.*

With rising panic, I rushed to the bathroom door and trapping the ball between door and frame, keeping the door closed by leaning back with all my weight, I began to tug with superhuman strength.

Unfortunately, it was just at this moment that the child's parents returned after their night out. So intent was I on trying to tear my head from the door-trapped toy that I didn't hear them enter the house. Attracted by all the huffing and puffing coming from the bathroom they made their way upstairs.

'Nigel, what on earth are you doing?'

I nearly died of fright.

When I realised who it was, I extricated myself from my extraordinary position and explained my dilemma. They, of course, fell about laughing; and when they had recovered about half-an-hour later they both grasped the end of the ball and with me bracing myself against the doorway we all pulled.

This time it worked. With a small explosion, like the sound of a cork emerging at speed from a bottle of champagne, the suction pad finally gave way and I, mightily relieved, was able to join in the general merriment.

All was not yet over, however. When I got home and was preparing to go to bed, I caught sight of myself in the bathroom mirror and to my horror there was a vivid red circle, about four inches in diameter, right in the middle of my forehead. It looked like a giant, bloodshot, third eye, a disfigurement particularly worrying because the next day I was expected to record an important interview with Clare Francis, the yachtswoman. The presence of the ghastly red blotch now threatened not only the film but the launch of my television career as a whole.

The next morning the horrible orb was, if anything, slightly worse. There was nothing to be done. Brushing the front of my hair as far down as possible I went to do the filming, making sure I always had a hand across my forehead as though deep in concentration.

'Have you got a headache?' Miss Francis eventually asked with concern.

I decided to tell her the truth and she roared with laughter. 'Don't worry,' she said, sympathetically. 'In fact I did exactly the same thing when I was playing with my son Thomas a couple of months ago.'

This made me feel better and when the crew had stopped laughing too we shot the interview so my face was only in profile.

Back in the office the 'affair of the plastic ball' became a running gag. I was first in line to cover any stories involving children, and film crews were briefed always to keep a careful eye on me: 'Don't let him play with any toys . . .' and 'Make sure he's supervised at all times . . .' etc., etc.

Generally my reception was quiet and slightly suspicious. The appointment of any new reporter was a fiercely argued issue because half the staff would like his or her face and manner and the other half would hate it.

It is also the kind of business which attracts petty rivalries and jealousies; whilst the successful candidate is catapulted to instant fame, the others — often from within the station staff itself — are as far away from it as ever.

In the reporters' scruffy room, with its peeling paint and short, dusty curtains and heaps of half-empty coffee cups, I sat at one desk but was told it belonged to Bruce; I moved to another but this one was apparently Jenni's; the third desk, I was courteously informed, was used by Tim; and I was asked to move from the fourth because this was Mike's desk.

At this point I spotted a fundamental flaw in the system; there was room for only four desks in the reporters' room whilst there were in fact five reporters, so I had to spend the next three years like a nomad constantly hopping from one temporarily unoccupied desk to another — most unsettling.

Bruce's desk was kept neat and very tidy. He was a dapper, well-spoken man always immaculately dressed, with a youthful, ageless face and a slight in-built resentment that he'd never been born into the peerage. He was the programme's suave, unflappable link-man who enjoyed the company of MPs and Chief Constables, and claimed he'd only ever used public transport once in his life and that was when he caught a bus from the Savoy to Harrods.

Jenni's desk was covered in an assortment of empty nail-varnish bottles and piled high with letters from men. She was a very attractive, fiercely ambitious girl who copresented the programme with Bruce and drew the kind of mail from admiring male viewers that would have brought a blush to the cheeks of Errol Flynn.

They were both very highly-regarded, experienced presenters whose ability to create a genuine loyalty amongst viewers kept the programme popular and successful and meant that there were frequent attempts to poach them by other programmes and rival companies.

They were also both extraordinarily relaxed in the studio. This I found quite disarming, particularly on my own first live piece of studio broadcasting: a modest, 45 second court report. Jenni straightened my tie maternally and gave me a wink and Bruce, seeing my terror, said: 'It's only television, you know, not brain surgery.' As the floor-manager counted us down from 30 seconds to transmission they were still laughing and chattering away without a care in the world.

Despite a severe attack of the 'bum and balls syndrome', I made it through my piece but afterwards got bad cramp in my fingers from gripping the legs of the desk in fear.

Nerves have peculiarly distorting effect; they tend to flatten the voice into a monotone and iron natural creases from the face like a fighter-pilot undergoing substantial gravitational pull.

'That was fine, lad,' said the programme's producer, Don,

*It's only television.*

emerging through a cloud of billowing pipe smoke like a soldier advancing through a heavy artillery bombardment in the trenches. 'But one tip — don't look so damned superior!'

I didn't like to puncture his belief in my confidence by telling him

89

that it had been one of the most frightening moments in my life so I simply nodded and said: 'Thank you.'

Don was also a highly-experienced television man with a great eye for a story but, unlike the others, he had a tendency to periods of high tension when he would pace up and down like a caged lion worrying himself to death. He always claimed the job had turned him grey. He wore huge woolly jumpers that could have covered a pantomime horse and he was the only man I've ever met who would absent-mindedly smoke both a cigarette and pipe simultaneously.

The secret of Don's success as a producer was that he had long ago grasped the idea that gathering news for the screen is as much a matter of logistics as journalistic values. Because of the time it took to organise and dispatch film crews at short notice, generally the stories best covered were those nearest base.

Planning a day's filming was a case of working back from the time of transmission — we were on air at 6 p.m. Even a very simple film could take three-quarters of an hour to edit, which puts us back to about 5 p.m. Film is shot in rolls of 400 ft, equivalent to 10 minutes worth of screen time, and by the time you've persuaded the processing technician to finish his tea in the canteen and come back to work, the best part of an hour was required for each roll to be processed in the station laboratories. That takes us back to 4 p.m. at least. Add an extra hour for visiting the gents, calming down the film editor waiting to cut the film, and Don knew that, as a rule of thumb, if his reporter wasn't back in the building with his film by 3 p.m. his ship was heading towards a lee shore.

Shooting the film could take 10 minutes or 10 days; but for the novice everything took much longer than it should.

The hardest task for me to master on location was the 'piece to camera' during which the reporter talks direct to the viewer. This is a knack; at first I spent hours writing down exactly what I wanted to say and memorising it until I was word perfect; later it became much more relaxed and spontaneous, like chatting to an old friend.

During my first week I did a 'piece to camera' 13 times. Every few seconds the image of a million people all sitting in their living rooms watching me flashed across my mind and I dried up. Applying my grandmother's advice now made things worse; the million people became a million cauliflowers and that was more horrific still. After getting through an entire packet of cigarettes, several bucketfuls of sweat and 300 feet of film I finally did an acceptable 'take' but Don said later that the knot of my tie looked squiffy and it was dropped.

Thanks to my experience in radio I found the interviews easier. This isn't always the case.

A friend of mine, Jim, started as a television reporter for the BBC in the Midlands. It was a very quiet news day and his producer wanted to do a story about the fact that most people living in Birmingham didn't know the name of their Bishop. Jim was told to take a film crew down to the cathedral and interview people in the street.

The story was working well — most people were unable to give the Bishop a name — when Jim approached a willowy figure wrapped in a large cloak.

'Excuse me, BBC TV, would you mind telling me the name of the Bishop of Birmingham please?'

'Sir,' said the face. 'I *am* the Bishop of Birmingham'.

Shortly afterwards, Jim retired as a reporter and eventually became a successful producer, legendary for his obsession for pre-filming research.

The trouble with my job was that there seemed precious little time or opportunity for research of any kind. We were on the road nearly every morning, frenzidly shooting films for transmission the same day; back in the newsroom, much bigger and even scruffier than the reporters' room, Don would sit like a general in a bunker under fire, barking out orders to the handful of 'off-camera' journalists assisting him and feverishly plotting the progress of his reporters and crews across Southern England.

He was a compulsive cartoonist and as he agonised over which stories were worth trying to cover and which were not, small mountains of brilliant sketches and caricatures scribbled out on scrap paper began to grow all over his desk.

After a few weeks my car was fitted with two-way radio so that I could keep in contact with the Bunker at HQ. Far from being an asset, I found the radio a positive nuisance. Its main function was to dish out more work; when rushing back to base with hundreds of feet of film in the boot it would pipe up with something like: 'On your way back pop off and do an interview with an old lady who's fitted her geriatric duck with an artificial leg would you old chap?' thus putting the whole day's work in jeopardy.

Shortly after the radio was installed I had just completed an interview with a local MP and was actually giving him a lift home when there was a deafening buzz and the voice of one of Don's minions floated over the airwaves.

'Nigel, you little worm, have you finished interviewing that boring old sod yet?'

I gave the MP a coy little smile and he tried to smile back.

I told the Bunker that I had indeed completed the interview and that the boring old sod was sitting right beside me now. There was a short, animal-like grunt and the radio went dead.

Even with the aid of radios, however, Don could never be certain exactly how the programme would eventually look. At any stage a

*Producer at work.*

story could disappear up the spout because of the myriad of trivial yet vital elements involved: the crew may never successfully rendezvous with the reporter (crews and reporters always travelled separately in case they had to be split during the day); they could get lost, marooned in traffic or given the wrong address; it might rain; film may be over- or under-exposed or ruined in processing; sound could be distorted.

Small wonder, then, that as the hours ticked by, the mountains of cartoons grew taller and the number of cigarettes burning in ash-trays doubled by the hour. When, at last, the programme was over and Don would say: 'It's a bloody miracle we ever get on the air', I knew he meant it.

The difficulties imposed on us by logistics were occasionally overcome by ingenuity.

On Budget Day we were in the reporter's room drinking coffee and discussing the prospects for the Chancellor's speech when Don bustled into the room scratching his head and as usual looking very worried.

This heralded work.

He stopped in the middle of the room, shuffled some papers, stared out of the window, lit another cigarette, and then began looking at us one by one. We all picked up telephones or started typing in the hope of looking busy.

Don finally padded over to me.

'What are you doing, Nige?'

'Well, I — '

'Ever been to a brewery?'

'I don't think I — '

'Pop down to that big brewery at Dorchester, will you? The Chancellor seems certain to stick at least a few pennies on the price of a pint, so go and point a camera at somebody to find out what any price increase will mean to the company.'

Before I had a chance to reply, Don was struck by a momentous thought about something else and, waving his arms in the air, he charged from the room like a cavalry trooper.

Now here was a problem. Dorchester was at least an hour and a half's drive away. The Chancellor's speech wasn't due to even begin until 3 p.m. To get any kind of reaction on film seemed impossible.

Bruce and Jenni, secretly thanking the Lord that Don hadn't chosen them, smiled sympathetically at me, enjoying my discomfort. Then Jenni suddenly banged her fist on the desk and told me she had the perfect solution.

93

'Go to Dorchester this morning and film six separate interviews with the brewery's managing director. In the first, get his reaction to no increase in the price of beer; in the second, his reaction to a penny increase; in the third his reaction to a two penny increase, and so on. It won't be more than fivepence a pint. Then, by the time you've driven the film back and it's been processed, the Chancellor will have announced his decision and you can use which ever interview is appropriate.'

I beamed at Jenni in grateful admiration and set off pronto for Dorchester. The brewery's managing director was a charming, intelligent man who knew a great deal about beer but not much about television. It took me the best part of half-an-hour to explain what I had in mind and when he'd grasped the idea he nearly had heart seizure. 'I can't do that,' he whined, trying to sound reasonable. 'I'll get horribly confused!'

After the usual persuasive mixture of flattery and oily encouragement, he agreed to give it a try.

Each of the six interviews was filmed completely separately and at first he did indeed become slightly confused. His responses ranged from: 'This is the best thing that's happened to the industry for years' for no increase at all, to: 'This is a total disaster for the industry and will mean widespread redundancies' for a fivepenny increase. He began by getting his tenses wrong, saying '*If* tuppence *is* put on . . . .' instead of the retrospective 'Now that tuppence *has been* put on . . .' but once we had ironed that one out he seemed to summon energy from a hitherto untapped reservoir and put on a very creditable performance.

He slipped up once more with the threepenny response: 'This is very bad news for an industry already facing at least some redundancies in the near future . . .' became confused with the fourpenny response: 'This is a very depressing and unfair attack on an industry already suffering great stress . . .' but after that there was no stopping him. By the time he reached the fivepenny increase response I felt he was on the verge of overdoing it: 'This is a tragedy, unparalleled in the great history of an industry built up by Englishmen who have sacrificed their lives for the future . . .' but judging by the way he was grinning like a Cheshire cat when we had switched off the camera he obviously thought it rather good.

'Was that all right?' he asked, flushed with excitement. 'If not I'm quite happy to do it again!'

'No, no that's fine.'

'What about a reaction to a sixpenny increase?'

'No, no, thank you.'

I urged the film crew to make a fast exit before the man offered to sing us a song and, three hours later, with the film safely processed, the Chancellor announced that twopence was to put on the price of a pint of beer. Everyone in the office was terribly impressed by my skill, except Don, who hadn't apparently appreciated the miracle and instead grumbled quietly on about how fivepence on a pint would have been a much better story.

On the other hand, sheer bad luck could equally easily torpedo the most immaculately prepared filming schedule.

A week after Budget Day, on a quiet morning when most of the programme was already filled, Jenni was giving me a most revealing account of a date she'd had with a Nicaraguan church warden from Reading when the hatchway linking the reporters' room with the newsroom suddenly slid open and Don's head popped through, straining like a tortoise trying desperately to eat a lettuce leaf just out of reach. 'Big story in Wiltshire. Another Bonnie and Clyde post office raid. Which of you two layabouts is going?'

Jenni and I pointed at each other simultaneously.

'Oh for God's sake, you idiots, we want this for tonight's programme, not next month!'

Jenni used her trump card. 'But Don,' she said sweetly, 'I've got a hair appointment in an hour's time. Surely you don't want me doing the show tonight like this?'

I was on my way.

Over the previous year there had been a large number of post office raids carried out by a young man and woman who had been dubbed by the local press Bonny and Clyde. What made them such a good running story was their sheer gall. On this occasion they had actually returned to a village post office they had raided only a few months before. Both times they had broken into the home of the postmaster and his wife, tied up the couple, then made off with the keys to the post office and its safe.

It was mid-day when I arrived in the village, with its two rows of neat little brick and thatched houses built from the dull grey local stone, separated by a wide stretch of long, shaggy grass. A goat, tethered to a tree, chomped away contentedly in the silence. There seemed nobody about. Hidden away in a small car park behind a pub I could just see the black and white chequered markings of the police mobile caravan that had been brought in to provide an office for the raid investigation.

I was relieved to see that Mike, the cameraman, was already there, taking shots of the street and the post office itself. We discovered a woman living nearby who had heard bangs and the sound of breaking glass in the night, so we interviewed her. A policeman helped us track down the detective leading the enquiry, and we interviewed him, too. Could we, I then enquired, talk to the postmaster himself?'

'He's a bit shell-shocked, but I agree it would be a good idea if he did talk to you. Go and try him.'

We hadn't much time so we went straight to the postmaster's bungalow just out of the village, and knocked on the front door. Eventually a dishevelled young man, presumably the son, appeared and asked us what the devil we wanted.

'I'm from the BBC, we'd like to . . .'

'Go away, you horrible little vulture.'

I've always like conversations that are short and to the point. I said I hoped he'd have a nice day.

In the back of his van, Mike unloaded the film from the camera magazine and into a small metal can. This is a tricky little process which must be done with both hands, film and can buried in a black, light-proof bag, and as always I was grateful that Mike could do it in about a minute, faster than any cameraman I've ever known.

'Don's been on the radio already, 'Mike told me. 'He says if we don't leave shortly we won't get this on the air.'

I ran back to my car, tossed the can of film into the boot, and began to search my pockets for the keys.

Just then I had a slight twinge that all was about to go horribly wrong.

Frantically, my fingers moved from pocket to pocket, hunting for the keys; from trouser pocket to jacket pocket to anorak pocket and back to trousers. When had I last used the keys? Racing, my thoughts retraced my steps, and suddenly the precise memory of what had happened appeared before me with awful clarity.

Along with the precious can of film, I had locked my keys in the boot of the car.

From the legs upwards my skin began to tingle, a sensation rather like climbing down into the icy water of a wintry sea. I tried to wrench open the boot, but not a millimetre would it move. I looked along the street to where Mike's big green van had been parked; it had already gone. Desperately, I stared up and down the pretty little village in search of inspiration.

Then I remembered the police caravan. I dashed over, tore open the door, and found two very large, helmetless constables drinking tea from steaming plastic mugs.

Rather shyly, I explained my circumstances.

The constables looked slowly at each other, and then back at me. The larger of the two, who had huge ginger sideboards which didn't quite join forces at the bottom of his chin, took a giant swig of boiling tea, and said: 'Oh dear, oh deary me.'

There was a short pause.

'So Mr Television Man has found himself in a spot of bother, has he?'

'I'm afraid so,' I confessed, feeling like someone just nabbed for shoplifting.

'And no doubt Mr Television Man wants the boys in blue to come and bale him out of trouble, is that it?'

'Something like that.'

Another swig of tea followed. His huge Adam's apple shot up and down like a yo-yo.

'Are you suggesting that an Officer of the Law should break into a car?'

The other started to chuckle at this. I shrugged.

'Oh dear, oh deary me.'

Then the two policemen sighed, slowly put on their helmets and followed me back to my car. The one with sideboards then miraculously produced a coil of thin wire from his pocket and began to stuff it vigorously into the boot lock whilst the other one alternately pushed and lifted, pushed and lifted.

I got the impression they may have done this before.

There was a great deal of exertion but the boot lock stubbornly refused to budge. Eventually the smaller constable, his helmet askew and very red in the face, shouted across the street to a young detective bearing a clipboard in the process of house-to-house enquiries. He joined us, taking the wire and jamming it back into the keyhole, saying: 'No, no Wilf, you must twist the end before pushing.' As he worked, both constables leapt on the boot simultaneously but although this looked dramatic, it again failed to produce any result.

Suddenly, from behind us, we heard a voice that sounded ominously like a senior policeman.

'All right, all right, what's all this about?'

Judging by the scrambled-egg on his hat, he was a Chief Inspector at least.

'Trying to help this lad open his boot, sir.'

*Police assistance.*

'Yes, I can see that, Wilf,' the Chief Inspector said frostily. He peered at us all slowly, in turn. Then, looking quickly over his shoulder, he said: 'Have you tried the old penknife trick?' He

98

produced a tiny knife from his pocket and, advancing like a man about to stab his victim to death, he attacked the keyhole with a vengeance. This time all three remaining officers climbed onto the boot and began bouncing up and down.

I suppose at any other time it might have been quite comical: four policemen, sweating and swearing as they tried to break into my car whilst the Bonny and Clyde gang made off with their sack of loot across the Wiltshire countryside. It didn't seem too amusing then, however, particularly when eventually they announced they had failed.

I rang Don from a call box. I think I hit him at a bad moment.

'You bastard, are you trying to crucify me? Do you realise that this is supposed to be my top story for tonight?'

I whimpered.

'What do we do?' he asked, after settling down and lighting a cigarette.

'Don, can you send someone over to my home to pick up the spare set of keys. They're in the top left drawer of my desk in the front room.'

'How do we get in?'

'The kitchen window should be open.'

Don absorbed this information without any audible enthusiasm.

'It'll take too long.'

'Use a dispatch rider.'

Another long silence.

'All right, you idiot,' Don said at length. 'Idiot, idiot, idiot.'

We made it — just. I got back a few minutes before five p.m. The film was rushed straight into processing and because it was only half a roll it was promised within half-an-hour. Waiting for it to emerge I wrote a commentary, and then a short introduction to the story which was typed straight onto teleprompt for Bruce to read live in the studio. At half-past-five the film was taken to a cutting room where a film editor sliced six shots together, including the two sections of interview. By ten-to-six the film was cut; it was laced up on the telecine machine from which, like the film in any home-movie projector, it awaited transmission. At 6 p.m. Bruce introduced the story and, sitting beside him in my shirt-sleeves just out of vision, I read the commentary.

I was surprised by the speed with which film could get on the air if it had to; yet over the coming months I realised that it was at times like these, with everyone under great pressure and some even near to panic, that the station performed at its best. In the last frenzied hour of activity before transmission all the stumbling blocks which had made life difficult earlier in the day were swept aside. Film editors, script girls, graphic designers, lighting engineers, reporters and presenters suddenly slipped into a high gear and performed minor miracles; it could be a most impressive operation.

At the end of each programme we would all sheepishly assemble in the newsroom for a post-mortem. Then the Manager arrived. He would then announce His verdict on the programme. If He liked it, there were visible signs of relief, with everyone talking at once and the Manager making a joke to roars of obliging laughter.

If He disapproved, however, a huge bubble of depression would fill the air, quickly followed by bitter recriminations. Afterwards we would all adjourn to the club bar where the back-slapping/arguments continued long into the night.

The following morning, 10 a.m. sharp, all those not already out filming would wearily gather once more in the newsroom and the whole ghastly process would begin all over again. Quite how, in the midst of all this daily confusion, Don actually managed to make good programmes I have never understood; but made they were. The station had an enviable reputation, consistently winning more viewers than its rivals, as well as a clutch of television awards; and if at times the system became so desperate that we felt like a herd of Gaderene swine charging over the cliff, then some divine intervention must have secretly supplied each of us with a parachute pack on our backs so that the journey from cliff-top to beach was not only eye-opening, it was beginning to look like fun, too.

# 7

It didn't take me long to realise that the success of my new work depended almost entirely on the cameramen.

In newspapers and radio the reporter worked alone; but now I found I had to rely on — and trust — a number of other people without whom films could never be made: the sound recordist, the laboratory staff, the film editor and the dubbing mixer. Above all, the cameramen had the fate of my films in their hands; if their work was poor, then so was mine.

Ron was a great cameraman for anyone new to the business. He was one of life's fixers. Over the years he'd found a way of overcoming nearly all the uncomfortable little problems which afflicted us when filming. If we wanted to slip into a hotel to get some shots of a VIP, Ron only had to tip the doorman a wink and within seconds we would be in at a hidden door at the back; if we wanted to book our car on the ferry to the Isle of Wight, and all spaces were reserved, Ron — somehow — got us a place. He had two unshakable characteristics: he knew everyone; and he was always late.

I passed an agonising half-an-hour with His Grace the Duke of Norfolk on the lawns of Arundel Castle in Sussex, waiting for Ron to arrive. I had worked hard to persuade His Grace to give me an interview, but he had insisted that we must do it quickly because he had to get to London for an important vote in the House of Lords. I gave an assurance that the cameraman would arrive within a few minutes; he was actually 15 minutes late already. Keeping His Grace busy with idle conversation, we walked out into the gentle morning sunshine which was splashed across the beautiful inner grass courtyard of the Castle, and watied.

Ron was not only a man for whom time meant very little; he was also well-known for his irreverence, and an apology to the Duke when eventually he did arrive would be the last thing on his mind. This made me more nervous still.

Gradually, the Duke of Norfolk, a polite but very firm man, grew quite visibly agitated. I'm supposed to be catching the next London train,' he said, starting at his watch and hopping excitedly from one foot to the other. 'I really must insist ...'

I did my best to placate him with grovelling phrases like: 'Any moment now, Your Grace, and your patience will be rewarded ...' and 'Craving Your Grace's indulgence, Your Grace ...' like a medieval courtier in danger of being beheaded.

At last Ron arrived, tooting his horn and blowing me a kiss.

My heart sank.

He shambled over, his hands in his pockets. I ran over to meet him. 'Don't you know how late you are?' I hissed. 'The Duke is furious ...'

Ron patted my cheek gently, gave me a wink and marched over to His Grace.

Oh God, I thought, cringing with embarrassment.

Ron put out his hand and produced a truly immortal phrase: 'Howdi Dook, how's tricks?'

I blanched.

The Duke of Norfolk turned slowly and faced Ron. Then, suddenly, his face burst into a grin. He grabbed Ron's hand and shook it violently. 'Hallo, Ron my old mate! Haven't seen you in years, how's it all going?'

The two men had filmed together many times before and knew each other like old friends. I slunk away, suitably chastised, to let them talk over old times.

When pushed, Ron had a fiery temper. Most of the time this was directed at a few of Don's minions in the Bunker who he saw as being out of touch with the day-to-day problems facing a film crew always on the road. Reporters were rarely expected to do more than one film a day, but whilst they beetled back to the office to get the film prepared for transmission, the crew would normally be sent on to a second job, or even a third. The crews thus spent most of their lives working at remote control, which often led to mis-understandings, angry exchanges and sometimes even threats of resignation.

What irked Ron and the other cameramen most was that they were so often working against large, well-equipped ITV crews who had secured very favourable working agreements and big expense

*Outnumbered.*

accounts. I once filmed an interview with a harbour master on the Isle of Wight with one cameraman and no other help at all. He did the filming and I held the microphone in one hand, a battery-light in the other while trying to remember what questions to ask. When we had finished, the harbour master stepped across to our ITV rivals who had already set up for a second interview. Much to his surprise he found that the BBC's two-man crew had now been replaced by an ITV crew of ten: a cameraman and his assistant, a sound recordist and assistant, two electricians, one production assistant, one director, one reporter and one driver.

In fact the picture and sound quality of both interviews turned out to be much the same, although in the ITV version the reporter did manage to remember all his questions.

In the provincial regions, the standard BBC news film unit normally consists of only three people: a reporter, a cameraman and a sound recordist. Whilst I always regarded it as the cameraman's privilege to grumble, it was usually the soundman who caused the trouble; it was the soundman who suddenly decided he had to change microphones after we had spent three-quarters of an hour setting up a shot; always the soundman who was too cold, too wet, too thirsty or too upset to concentrate. Reporters always directed their own films, which left us with a great deal of work but plenty of freedom and control, too.

Ron and I were once dispatched to London to film a demonstration by dockyard workers whose jobs were in danger from Government defence cuts. Hundreds of thousands of men, amongst them workers from the Naval Dockyard at Portsmouth, gathered on Clapham Common to hear speeches before setting off on a march to the House of Commons where they were to lobby MPs.

The filming on the Common went well, and just after the long, sad column of men set off on the march to Westminster, Ron and I began looking for a taxi so that we could get there before them and so film their arrival. It was a hot summer's day and we stood on the dusty roadside under a beating sun for over half-an-hour in search of a cab. Across the road the ITV crews were winking patronisingly at us as they stepped into their chauffeur-driven limousines.

After waiting another 10 minutes we tried to wave down a bus. Then we walked half-a-mile to the tube. The underground journey involved changing trains twice but, as it was mid-day, services were infrequent. Ron had become very silent indeed which was a bad sign. When we finally arrived at the Commons, exhausted under the weight of our gear, to see the march already beginning to break up and the ITV crews licking ice-creams in the back of their cars, Ron started huffing and puffing like an old geyser.

'What a f... cock-up!' he said softly. If it had been physiologically possible for steam to emerge from his ears, this would have been the moment of its appearance. 'I'm never working for this f... organisation again.'

Ron never has resigned.

Most of our cameramen were prepared to go to great physical discomfort in pursuit of a good shot. We were making a film about a vintage Rolls-Royce on one occasion and discussing how best to get a moving, or 'tracking' shot of the car tootling along the road. The cameraman suggested that I should drive my own car just ahead and he could sit in the boot shooting the Rolls coming up behind. This we did. Unfortunately, we were driving along a country track full of pot holes and every time I hit a bump, the roof of the boot came cracking down on the poor fellow's head as he was filming. Since we had no means of communication, I continued to drive and he continued to film until we stopped some miles later to discover that long red bumps had popped up all over the cameraman's head so that it resembled a Second World War sea mine.

The shot itself was rock steady.

Not long after this another of our cameramen inadvertantly filmed the process of falling flat on his face, which provided one of the most extraordinary pieces of film I have ever seen.

He was a small, lightweight man and I asked him if he could go along to a nearby RAF airfield and get a shot of a huge Chinook helicopter touching down on landing; it was part of a feature about the RAF we were compiling and all that was required was that actual moment of contact between the wheels of the helicopter and the ground.

He pottered along to the airfield on his own at the allotted time for what should have been a very quick, simple task; but what we had both failed to consider was the enormous down-draught of the Chinook's two vast rotor-blades on landing. The cameraman was actually blown completely off his feet and thrown to the ground, but valiantly he kept filming, and the result was classic.

The shot began with a perfectly sharp image of the huge helicopter descending. The camera was held beautifully steady as the machine dropped gracefully to mother earth; then suddenly, as the down-draught hit the cameraman, the shot went berserk. The helicopter disappeared as the picture careered crazily about the sky; then there was a handful of startled faces, fuzzy and upside down, then bags more sky, several telegraph poles at extraordinary angles, two upside-down hangars followed by huge pieces of grass rushing towards us at high speed.

By now the cameraman was flat on his back, but still he kept filming. A giant army boot shot into focus. Then a grossly distorted face peered into the lens of the mute camera, mouthing 'Are you all right?' silently and then nodding violently. There then followed the long struggle to stand up, interspersed with a variety of buildings, trousers, cars, telegraph poles and acres more sky, until at last the helicopter reappeared safely on the ground and slowly came back into focus.

The shot lasted for several minutes and included virtually everything visible on the airfield except that one, vital moment of the Chinook touching-down.

Most of the cameramen, of course, had seen it all before. It seemed impossible to surprise or shock them, although on rare occasions they would succumb to the events they were in the process of filming, often those you might least expect.

We had been called to the scene of a violent robbery in which an elderly couple had been beaten up by a gang of youths and their home ransacked. The house was in chaos — furniture torn apart, beds overturned, even wall paper stripped off. An old sepia photograph of the couples' parents had been tossed on the floor and stamped on. It was a small, cold, poor house, one of a blackened-stone terrace, containing scarcely anything worth stealing. Ron took a few shots inside and some exteriors, whilst chattering away to his soundman Peter. When they had finished they packed away their gear in the car and waited whilst I called the police station. I could hear them laughing over some old joke.

On the 'phone I asked the police if we could film an interview with the couple in hospital. This was out of the question; detectives were still waiting for them to recover sufficiently to give more detailed descriptions of their attackers.

When I told this to Ron he said: 'I know old Freddie, the administrator up at the hospital, nice chap. Come on, he'll let us in.'

I frowned. 'Ron, they haven't even let the police in yet.'

Ron winked at me with that infuriatingly confident style of his. He was always smiling, self-assured, with his long, dark hair swept back over the collar of the old flying-jacket he used to wear.

Before I had a chance to stop him he had driven off to the hospital, and I stood there, cursing him, until I realised had no choice but to follow. A television reporter without a film crew isn't much use to anyone.

I was praying that on just this one occasion Ron would be wrong. He wasn't, of course. I caught up with him in the lobby of the hospital, where he was deep in merry conversation with a tall, thin man I assumed to be Freddie. They were slapping each other on the back and from time to time the rows of pale, dazed patients awaiting some kind of attention would sit up with a jerk, startled, as the air was filled with roars of laughter.

Eventually, now winking madly, Ron walked over to me and said: 'It's fine, we can go now, before the police arrive,' and despite myself I couldn't help admiring his style.

106

We took the lift up to the seventh floor, and hurried through a long series of dark corridors and past a waiting police photographer who still hadn't been given permission to see the couple. I was just chuckling to myself about how pleased the Bunker would be that we had stolen a march on the police when I followed Ron into a small room, and there they were.

The sight of that poor, desperate old couple took my breath away.

Their faces were an appalling mass of colour, of black and blue, but vivid red and purple, too, where they had been punched and kicked and cut. The old man had an obscene black swelling, as large as a cricket ball, which puffed out one cheek; along the other side of his face was a long, thin black line, crossed with tiny stitches, like a railway line on a map, where his skin had been ripped by a knife or a piece of glass.

I recognised his wife as a woman only because of her hair. Her eyes and mouth had completely disappeared in a sea of swollen cuts and bruises.

They had left their beds and gone downstairs and disturbed the robbers at work.

For several moments we were so shocked we didn't say anything; then I tried to explain why we were here and they nodded their understanding and croaked out a few words. I was amazed by their composure and fortitude; there was no anger, no bitterness, just a quiet resignation.

Ron was nearly in tears.

The couple told us quietly that they would like to be interviewed so that everyone could see what had happened. We weren't enthusiastic but even I knew that you shot the film first then asked the questions about it later.

Ron worked in total silence.

Later, back in the office, I showed the film to Don. I was afraid he'd consider the shots too horrific to screen at tea-time.

'That's just what we should be showing, at tea-time or any time,' he said quickly. Even he, though, was unable to disguise his shock.

Ron's bold approach to camera work made him the ideal working companion when filming the unpredictable. If we were covering an angry demonstration, or violent scenes on a picket-line, or a punch-up amongst film crews jostling for best position at a news conference then — providing he arrived somewhere near the right time — Ron was the fellow to have at hand.

The station's other main cameraman was Mike, a small, youthful and blond man famed for his careful, precise and imaginative film work. Unlike Ron, he was quiet, polite, very efficient and equipped with the smallest bladder I have ever known in any man.

*Ron and Mike.*

Mike knew by heart the exact location of nearly every public convenience in the South of England. Occasionally, when filming, people would ask if we'd like coffee, and if I was with Mike, these words would fill me with gloom. After the intake of even one modest cup, the following two hours filming would be interrupted every five minutes by Mike saying: 'Excuse me for a moment, folks,' and disappearing.

The fact that a single cup of coffee appeared to produce several pints of output puzzled him as much as it did us, a topic which provided hours of fascinating speculation.

Mike was an exceptionally hard worker. He worked from early morning to late at night, and he would never complain. Apart from his bladder, there was only ever one consistent interruption to the working day, and that involved a curious little habit which took me several months to understand. The first time it occurred was when I was following Mike in his big green van to a location. He suddenly pulled up on the side of the road, leapt out and feverishly ripped up handfuls of long grass. These he stuffed into big paper bags. After a few minutes of this he jumped back into the van and we proceeded.

I hadn't known Mike long and didn't like to ask him about this odd ritual. Then it happened several times again, usually when we had paused in filming. A glazed expression would pass across his face, and then he'd say: 'Excuse me folks,' and hurry off to ravish any patches of green grass nearby.

It was only months later that I had the opportunity to ask his soundman, Tim, for an explanation. 'Didn't you know?' Tim asked in a hushed whisper, as though discussing some personal hygiene problem, or terminal illness, 'Mike picks grass for his daughter's pet rabbit.'

Over the years Mike had learnt to make great sacrifices for television. He could be called on at any time, at any place, and whilst this rule applied to the reporters as well, there were generally only two cameramen available whilst there were five of us.

Over the years this way of life had produced in Mike a stomach of cast-iron. I once went out into the Solent with Mike and Tim to make a film about the unloading of Christmas supplies for the three men who manned the famous Needles lighthouse on the western tip of the Isle of Wight. We set off on a motor-launch from Lymington and our first mistake was to accept some sandwiches, made by the skipper's helpful wife, which were stuffed with cold, greasy bacon.

Because of the clash of conflicting currents, the area of water around the Needles rocks is notoriously rough even in calm weather. Today, as we sat up on deck in a chilly sea breeze, I could see heavy black storm clouds moving up from the south over the dark, shadowy silhouette of the island and as I stared the breeze began to stiffen.

We had to wait some time for the supply boat to arrive, and as the swell grew I noticed that Tim had turned green.

Eventually, he grabbed a bucket, threw down his equipment, and retreated to the seat in the stern of the boat, where he curled up like a hibernating hedgehog and went completely incommunicado.

As the wind grew, the boat began to heave and twist. With poetic justice, the skipper's wife, the cause of the problem, also armed herself with a bucket and battened herself down below decks. Then the skipper himself, leaning over the side on some feeble pretext of wanting to examine some chipped paintwork, was violently sick. In so doing he broke the cardinal rule of all sailors, viz. never be sick into wind. By now there was a force eight blowing and the skipper's semi-digested pieces of greasy bacon were flung back at us on deck like grape-shot from a cannon.

By this time, Tim was heaving regularly into his bucket; and I'm afraid the sight of all this surplus bacon made me fell so ill that I went astern and joined Tim on the opposite end of the bench. With a huge lurch, the boat suddenly rolled violently and Tim's half-full bucket slid down the bench towards me. It arrived just in time, and I was able to finish using it just as the boat began to roll back and the bucket returned along the bench to its original position. This see-saw action continued for some time, each of us timing ourselves exactly to hit the bucket as it zoomed down towards us.

Mike, who incidentally had eaten twice as many greasy bacon sandwiches as the rest of us, remained cheerfully unaffected by all this, despite the fact that many cameramen, having to concentrate on a moving horizon through a moving camera lens, are prone to seasickness. In fact the sight of all of us dying seemed to positively perk the wretched man up. His resulting pictures were outstanding; but it's the sight of that smiling, happy face asking: 'What's up folks, spot of the dicky tummy?' which will remain in my memory for ever.

# 8

At first, she was nothing more than a shimmering, black dot on a distant, misty horizon. Even by the time our lumbering old transport aircraft had flown us over her stern, she still looked a small and curiously inoffensive ship, lost in the huge greyness of the North Sea.

We were about to land on the deck of the biggest and most powerful naval vessel afloat, the American aircraft carrier the USS *Nimitz*, en route for a courtesy visit to Portsmouth at the head of a NATO Task Force.

The transport plane suddenly dropped down, like a bird, which made me feel a little giddy. Flying has never been one of my favourite pastimes and the prospect of landing on an aircraft carrier did not leave me whooping for joy.

What slightly surprised me was that after 50 years the basic landing and take-off mechanism on carriers had hardly changed. Whether it be a supersonic jet fighter or an ageing aerial workhorse, the descending aircraft hangs a small hook from its tailplane and as it touches down the hook catches a steel rope lying flat across the flight deck and, with luck, brings aircraft and passengers to a stop.

Experiencing a landing like this is a most peculiar sensation and is not recommended for anyone with a weak stomach or loose-fitting false teeth. At one moment you are travelling through the air at high speed; the next you have stopped dead. You, the passenger, tend to bend violently around your middle at this moment, rather like a long piece of rubber, and your extremities, viz. top of head and tip of toes, suddenly find themselves in unexpected contact.

The *Nimitz* is a fantastic ship. It is nuclear-powered, so it can run for 13 years without any kind of refuelling. It has nearly 100 aircraft on board, compared with the eight aeroplanes carried, for example, by a British carrier like HMS *Invincible*, and a crew of 6,000.

It is a small, floating city, with its own chapels and mortuaries, muggings, drug-addicts and murderers. Stepping on board was like entering a bizarre new world.

With a visit to Portsmouth imminent, Don had cheekily asked the US Navy if they would fly a film crew to the *Nimitz* to shoot a preview of the ship. The US Navy, being the US Navy, had said, 'Sure, buddy, we'll pick you up in one of our very own 'planes at a military airfield, at your convenience.'

The officers on board were very friendly, courteous and, unlike their British equivalents, only too keen to tell us about their ship and its capabilities. Morale, we were told, was at last beginning to pick up after the disastrous attempt to rescue the American hostages in Iran had been launched from the *Nimitz* by helicopter, just a few months before.

Luncheon was repulsive. I have eaten in many a Royal Navy mess, where the food and wines are generally very good and all is impeccably served by scores of servile ratings dashing about the place like slaves in Caesar's palace. Here the food was in self-service trays and, following everyone else's example, I picked up one slice of cold liver (I hate cold liver), one portion of cold chips (I hate cold chips) and one doughnut (I love doughnuts) all on one plate. This was served with a glass of iced black tea.

We had been told that the Admiral of the Task Force, a very senior American naval officer, would be available after lunch for a news conference. Just as I was struggling with a forkful of doughnut and cold chips, the door of the mess swung open and in stepped a middle-aged man in an old boiler suit and a baseball hat.

On one side of his face there was a long streak of oil.

'Hi! How's it going, kiddoes?' he asked us all en masse. I thought I detected a slightly wild look in his eyes.

We all gave an embarrassed grunt, and he said: 'Anything you need?' We all shook our heads politely and he said: 'Lunch OK?' We all nodded, trying not to throw up, and with a small smile and a little presidential-type wave he stepped through the gangway, gave his head a mighty crack on the plate-head above, which knocked his baseball hat squiffy, and disappeared.

A ghastly thought crossed my mind and, turning to my American companion, I asked: 'That wasn't the Admiral by any chance, was it?'

The American nodded wearily. 'That was him.'

'But what about our news conference?'

*The Admiral's 'news conference'.*

'That was it.'

The journey home was more bizarre still. Catapulted back in the general direction of Southern England in our little transport plane it should have been quite straight forward. However, after about half-an-hour in the air we started descending and suddenly found ourselves landing at a military airfield. This turned out to be the huge US airbase of Mildenhall in East Anglia, and when we asked the pilot why we had landed he looked very sheepish indeed. Scratching his left leg along the tarmac like a sick dog, he said: 'We've run out of gas.'

'How could that happen?' we asked in amazement.

The answer was pathetic in its simplicity.

'Forgot to fill up before we left the *Nimitz*.'

We waited by the aeroplane for an hour and nothing happened. Eventually the pilot went off to demand petrol. He returned a few minutes later.

'They won't give us any gas.'

'Why not?'

'Gas wagon's bust.'

Now this was a little difficult to swallow. Here we were, en route from the American Navy's biggest ship, via one of the American Air Force's biggest bases in Europe, and we still couldn't get any bloody petrol to get home.

After another hour the pilot wandered off again. He fared no better.

'They're having problems mending the gas wagon.'

Someone said: 'Sod the bloody gas wagon' and we all clapped. Then someone else came up with an idea: there was an RAF fighter base less than five minutes flying time away at Cottishall — surely the RAF would have some spare gas?

The pilot radioed Cottishall and by the time we arrived a petrol tanker was already in position on the edge of the runway. As we climbed out of the transport plane an RAF officer with a swanky little moustache strode up to us.

'What's the problem, chaps?'

Our American pilot was nowhere to be seen, so I tried to explain.

'But why didn't you fill up with petrol on the *Nimitz*?' the RAF officer asked, puzzled.

'Forgot.'

He made a small gurgling noise and began to stroke his moustache like a wet otter.

114

'But what was wrong with Mildenhall?'

'Gas wagon bust.'

The RAF man frowned for a moment, then, as the truth dawned, he was scarcely able to contain his delight. With a quick nod and a little squeal of pleasure, he ran off excitedly; no doubt he went straight to the officer's mess to report the news gleefully.

Don enjoyed the *Nimitz* film so much that the very next week he sent us on an even more hazardous naval mission.

Like most of Don's stories, it sounded easy enough.

He breezed into the reporters' room looking full of beans and with a small smile twitching over the lips which gripped his cigarette like a vice. This did not bode well. Don was cheerful, Don was smiling. Observing these early warning signs, I withdrew into a hunched position like a tortoise sensing danger and began to type furiously.

'Busy, Nige?' he asked, craning over my shoulder to discover I was writing total gibberish.

'Well, I . . .'

'Liked your *Nimitz* material. Good story, fascinating insight. The Manager was impressed.'

'Thank you, I . . .'

'Ever been winched down from a helicopter onto the deck of a destroyer at sea?'

'I don't think I . . .'

'Be at the Naval Air station at Leigh-on-Solent at 4 a.m. sharp tomorrow. Good luck.'

This story centred around not an American carrier, but a large Russian cruiser steaming up the Channel on a route which took it much closer to our coastline than any other Russian military ship in recent history. The Soviets were being shadowed by a Royal Navy destroyer; we were to be dropped by helicopter onto the destroyer and make a short film about how the shadowing operation was being carried out.

We arrived at Leigh-on-Solent early on a very cold morning, in the middle of a gale. As I parked the car and clambered out into the howling wind, huge black clouds were being bundled across the sky. I smiled grimly to myself; there'd be no flying in this.

Thinking of mugs of hot tea and plates piled high with eggs and bacon that we could now go off and find in one of Portsmouth's early morning cafes, Ron, Peter and I walked into the airfield's operations rooms to pay our respects and announce that we were on our way.

'Pity about the weather,' I told the officer-in-charge.

'Pity? No pity about it, lad, you'll have a wonderful trip!'

I looked at Ron; Ron looked at me.

'You don't mean we are flying in this?'

'Of course we are, lads. Here are your life jackets.'

I had never flown in a helicopter before. I didn't like aeroplanes. Helicopters, I suspected, would be more frigtening still. The prospect of taking my first trip in a hurricane and then being winched down onto a heaving destroyer did not inspire me.

A second officer arrived, all hearty, red-faced and with beaming smiles, to give us a briefing.

'If the chopper ditches in the sea you are not to try to get out until the cockpit is completely submerged and you are sure the blades have stopped rotating,' he said comfortingly. 'If you try to escape with the blades still going round you will be decapitated.' Here he gave a curious little giggle. 'Not the sort of thing Head Office want to hear about ...'

More giggles.

'Head Office ... that's a joke.'

I tried to smile but the muscles on my face had already apparently taken on rigor mortis. Peter laughed; Ron kicked him under the table.

'Whilst still inside the cabin,' continued the buffoon, still chuckling, 'on no account must your life jacket be inflated. If you do inflate it you will simply float straight to the roof of the cockpit and then be unable to swim down to get to the door.' More grins. 'You will then either drown or suffocate. OK?'

'OK.'

His words went round and round in my mind as we walked out onto the tarmac and climbed into the Wessex parked in black silhouette against the brightening, wind-torn sky. My knees were trembling. Ron and Peter were struggling with our filming equipment. How we would cope with all that on the winch down I didn't dare imagine.

116

We were strapped into our seats just a few feet from the huge side-door of the aircraft, which was left open, and issued with helmets.

'They *should* stop you being knocked unconscious, OK?'

'OK.'

The noise of the Wessex's exhaust, positioned just outside our cabin door, was deafening and prevented any kind of conversation. With a lurch, the Wessex leapt into the air, tossed upwards by the winds sweeping in from the sea. We banked sharply, so that I was hanging down towards the door, and beat off over the Solent.

I tried closing my eyes, but that made things worse. I looked at Ron. He was terrified, too. In both our minds we were already wording our letters of resignation.

After only a few minutes in the air, the helicopter shuddered and suddenly dipped down towards the white-topped waves. Its engines roared. With another sharp bank, it turned away from the wind and seemed to be heading back to the land.

Something was wrong.

I looked at the helicopter's winchman squatting by the door. Was I imagining it, or did he, too, look scared? He caught my eye. To my horror he slowly slid his forefinger across his throat, as though it were being cut.

Then he gave me an exaggerated thumbs-down sign.

As if under hypnosis, I repeated his actions, and grimly he nodded in reply.

The mission was aborted. We were all going to die.

I had once read how the imminence of death plays awful tricks on the human consciousness. Apparently, the individual is convinced in his own mind that whilst everyone around him must inevitably be killed, he, somehow, will survive. This wasn't so in my case. I was convinced in my own mind that whilst everyone around him might survive, I, inevitably, would be killed.

I tried to remember our emergency briefing, but the jolly, giggling face of the officer dominated everything. He was laughing now, laughing at my decapitated head going round and round and round on the end of a propellor blade. Ron was laughing, too, as he slowly suffocated at the top of the cabin with his life-jacket inflated. The images spun round in my mind, laughter, waves, Ron laughter,

*Convinced of non-survival.*

Head Office, Don's pipe, laughter, laughter, laughter.

I realised someone was shaking me. I could hear voices. I opened my eyes, slowly, agonisingly.

It appeared we had landed. Safely.

'Are you all right?' shouted a face. It belonged to the winchman. He looked concerned.

'Yes, yes, I'm fine. Have we crashed?'

He looked mystified. 'Crashed? No, we're back at base. Radio wasn't working properly. Regulations say we mustn't fly without the radio working properly.'

I stumbled out and tottered back to the operations room. The helicopter engines began to throb slower and at last were cut. I watched from the window as Ron and Peter unloaded the gear.

I was alive.

I had some coffee, which helped me recover, and after a time Ron and Peter appeared, smiling but pale. 'Blimey,' said Ron, under his breath. 'That was a real scrotum-tightener.' This was a reference to the physiological reaction of the male sex to danger.

Even under these circumstances, I couldn't resist the temptation.

'Don't be feeble, Ron. We'd only lost radio contact — surely that wasn't enough to scare you?'

I thanked God quietly when we were told that there was no other aircraft available and the story was abandoned.

A few weeks later I was on another assignment when I bumped into Jo, a cameraman from our rival ITV station. He had been filming in a navy helicopter at Portland Harbour in Dorset a few years before. The chopper had ditched. There were five men on board. 'I was sitting up next to the pilot,' Joe explained. 'He and I managed to scramble out into the water and were safe. The other three men died.'

●　　●　　●

My life as a television reporter changed completely the day a young pig tried to bite off my testicles.

It was one of those loony stories that only regional television would dare cover. It was Valentine's Day and, much against my better judgement, Don had sent me to film a pig that had apparently become lovesick.

The pig was called Pinky, a 'pampered porker', as we described her in the film, and she was cared for in great luxury by a farming family who kept her in a greenhouse and fed her beautifully-prepared food and even took her for walks every day.

See what I mean?

What clinched it as an idiotic Valentine's Day story was that this wretched Pinky was having trouble finding a mate. Apparently she seemed quite interested in sex but just couldn't quite find the right fellow. The script lines, as you can imagine, wrote themselves, i.e. 'Pinky the poor pampered porker, pining for passion,' etc., etc.

119

I suggested Pinky was probably Lesbian, but this failed to amuse her loving family.

We filmed Pinky being pampered, and as a final thought I innocently jumped into her pen for a short 'piece to camera'.

As I was talking the animal began to attack my groin.

*Pinky, the poor pampered porker . . .*

At first, being a true professional, I tried to complete the sentence; but as Pinky's devilishly sharp little teeth worked their way up my leg and dangerously close to my vital components, I started leaping about like someone demented and finally decided to quit whilst I was still in one piece.

Pinky sensed my concern and like the shark, Jaws, she made one final agonising lunge at my upper thigh. I leapt into the air and vaulted over the side of the pen.

Despite my squeals and shouts of pain, Ron had thought I was joking and kept filming. As I flew overhead I could hear him laughing.

When I picked myself off the floor I realised there was blood all over the greenhouse. Already my leg was swelling up into a series of big black bruises and one of my fingers had been torn open.

Ron, trying now to stifle his laughter, bandaged me up and sped me back to the office where a doctor was waiting with a series of very unpleasant injections. After more bandages, I was able to limp back into the reporters' room.

Jenni seemed very concerned. She sat me down and gave me a coffee. But when I told her what had happened she turned away to the window so I couldn't see her face, and started spluttering. Then her shoulders went up and down like a pair of bellows and I realised she was laughing.

'Sorry, Nigel, but it's just so *funny!*'

Just then Don burst in. He was giggling uncontrollably. Without even looking at me, he said: 'Jenni, come and have a look at this, it's the funniest piece of film I've ever seen,' and the two of them shot out at high speed, leaving me alone with my throbbing pain.

I could hear the guffaws of laughter floating down the corridor.

Later Don returned to the reporter's room, still giggling so much that he put a cigarette into his mouth the wrong way round and tried to light the tip. The room was filled with a foul smell.

'It's going to slay them,' he said at last, wiping the tears from his eyes. 'It'll really slay them!'

'Slay who?' I enquired.

'Our viewers, of course.'

I was horrified.

'You're not intending to show that out-take of me being attacked by Pinky on the programme?'

Don looked down at me as though I was mad. 'Of course I am, idiot, it's the only bit of the film *worth* showing.' And, still chortling away, he wandered out. I had never seen him so happy.

The film caused such hilarity amongst our viewers that it was shown again at the end of the week. It was shown again, and then repeated. The comic effect was heightened by the fact that in his hurry to lose the swearing I had uttered, as Pinky's teeth had sunk into my flesh, the dubbing engineer had in fact bleeped out the wrong words. The sequence thus went something like this: 'God Almighty, this pig is having a go at my farting \*\*\*, shit it really \*\*\*.' I think this may well be the first recorded occasion a BBC reporter has ever used such words on air. Then, hastily redubbed, it was sent up to London and transmitted on a network programme.

The episode with Pinky became the bane of my life. Everywhere I went members of the public stopped me and made appalling jokes. Never again could I be taken seriously as a television journalist.

It was ghastly.

The day after the film had first been transmitted I walked into a shop to buy a newspaper. I noticed with some alarm that the man behind the till was eyeing me with an unpleasant smirk. I tried to look inconspicuous but he kept staring. I joined the queue of people waiting to pay and as I moved slowly towards the till the man winked — repulsively.

When I finally reached him, he leant over the counter, poked me in the stomach, and said: 'I am right, aren't I?'

I looked around at the other customers, smiling uncomfortably.

'I beg your pardon?'

'I am right, aren't I?' he repeated, and then putting his hands up to his face he grunted, snarled like a pig, then fell about laughing.

'Could I have this paper, please?'

He ignored my question.

'Does the name Pinky mean anything to you? Eh? Eh?

More laughter.

I smiled and nodded. 'Yes it does.'

He shouted down the shop to his wife stacking magazines on a rack.

''Ere, Ethel, this is that geezer who had his goolies nipped by the porker on the box last night!'

Ethel screamed with laughter. Some of the other customers joined in. Others, in a hurry, were getting angry.

'Look, may I pay for this paper, please?'

He poked me in the stomach again.

"'Ere, I tell you something, mate.'

'What?'

'I bet you don't like people mentioning that, do you? Eh? Eh?'

I cursed Don.

Shopping expeditions became a nightmare.

With the pig-biting incident constantly being repeated on national television, things gradually became worse, not better.

A few weeks later I was sent to make a film at a local prison. It was a place well-known for its high proportion of violent young inmates, and I arrived at the main gate with a feeling of trepidation. I was escorted through three sets of locked doors before even entering the main courtyard, and to reach the Governor's office in the administrative block in the centre of the compound I was taken through an outer locked door, an inner locked door, a locked corridor door and, finally, through a huge, locked, oak door that was also bolted top and bottom.

The Governor, a small, very stern-looking man with a cropped hair-cut, was hunched behind an enormous desk on the other side of the room. He watched me coldly as I stepped forward and nervously introduced myself. It was an oppressive, daunting atmosphere and I felt trapped.

Solemnly, he began to tell me about the prison but, as he spoke, I noticed that the veins in his neck had started to bulge, as though his whole body was under some kind of strain. Then his broad, tough frame began to shake, and small tears began to roll down his pale, chubby cheeks.

I thought he was crying. Then, as I watched, I realised he, too, was laughing, laughing hysterically.

'I expect the first thing you would like to do,' he managed to say, whilst desperately biting his lip and trying to control himself, 'is to visit our prison farm.'

This was puzzling. 'Prison farm, sir?'

'Yes,' he said, his face now swelling out like a dam about to break, so that it became much bigger than ever it was designed to be, 'yes, the prison farm . . . lots of pigs on the farm!' With this the dam finally gave way and he bent double with roars of laughter.

I have a feeling Pinky will be with me for the rest of my career.

• • •

123

As life on the road became more and more — what's the polite word? — stimulating, then life in the office became more interesting, too, as I gradually won over the confidence of my new colleagues.

Every Christmas the studio crew organised an 'in-house' video to be shown to the staff on the night of the office Christmas party. It came in the form of a half-hour pantomime, recorded in the studio one evening a few days before, and was intended to be a clever satire about life on the station, with the intention of embarrassing the manager as much as possible. Actually, most years it rapidly deteriorated into a drunken farce which was extremely difficult to understand, particularly for anyone sober.

After my success with Pinky, I was cast as Big Tex who towards the end of the story is attacked and bitten in the downtown saloon bar by Lovely Lil (Jenni). No expense was spared in this lavish drama and I was supplied with a magnificent cowboy outfit, with a huge pair of cowherd trousers, the size of two oil pipelines sewn together, along with a vast ten-gallon hat.

Unfortunately, my appearance didn't take place until the last act so I repaired to the BBC Club bar and awaited my call. There I bumped into Steve and Ian from local radio, who screamed with laughter when they saw what I was wearing and asked me if I had just been reading the news. Then things settled down for some serious drinking.

After an hour or two of this I slipped into a deep sleep, propped up in the corner of the bar.

I awoke some time later amidst a pungent smell of burning, and jumping up I saw that the cigarette I had been smoking when I had dozed off had fallen onto my beautiful chequered Texan shirt and produced a large black hole. Trying to hide this in my hand I dashed down to the studio to find everyone asking where the hell I had been. Lurching onto the studio floor, I tripped over two camera cables and fell flat on my face twice in 20 seconds, then started muttering totally incomprehensible gibberish whilst Lovely Lil did her best to keep me upright and at the same time bite my leg.

It must have been the lack of food, but what happened next is something I can only relate through the testimonies of a reliable witness.

*Big Tex.*

Now at most television stations there exists a very small 'presentation' studio where one person, operating completely alone, can put himself on air. It's a simple process if you know how to do it, involving the flicking of a number of switches, hidden from the public's view in a small trench in the desk. It's normally used by, say, a late-night newsreader broadcasting the closing headlines long after everyone else has gone home.

That night, with the panto at last safely in the can, one of the newsroom journalists was locking-up when he heard a strange, demonic chuckle coming from the darkened presentation studio. Nervously, he crept down the corridor and peered in; there was an American cowboy, his chest sticking through a large black hole in his shirt and his ten-gallon hat lurching precariously from the back of his head, just about to sit down in front of the camera.

To this day he swears that the cowboy drunkenly hissed at him to get lost whilst he put himself on air and related to the late night viewing audience a joke about an Irishwoman who had three breasts.

Thank God! the fellow had enough wits about him to pull out a few plugs.

# 9

'The Manager wants to see you.'

Enid was smiling sympathetically. She had a wide, warm smile, a maternal, knowing smile. For years she had been the ultra-efficient newsroom secretary, keeping the programme ticking over day-by-day, keeping track of people and money and times and dates so that she usually just managed to hold back the tide of chaos and confusion which constantly threatened to engulf us all.

Enid was aware of everything, and with her knowledge she could, for example, predict trouble brewing. She was a reliable ally.

'He wants to see me?' This was unusual. The Manager was an ethereal creature usually seen only at programme post-mortems or occasionally floating up and down a corridor before melting away into His huge office.

Enid was normally so busy that she would be carrying on about 16 separate conversations simultaneously; today she was ominously giving me all her attention.

'He wants to see you.'

'But why?' I asked nervously.

'Because of this,' said Enid, holding up a copy of the *News of The World*.

She opened the paper on page two; and there, across the page, ran the banner headline: HOW THE BBC STOPPED THE TRAFFIC.

'Oh God,' I snivelled.

'Quite,' said Enid.

The article referred to a film I had made a few days before about a group of residents living alongside a small, congested main road who were organising a campaign for the building of a by-pass. The traffic outside their homes was so heavy, so slow-moving, so noisy and so foul-smelling that their lives had become wretched.

The idea, of course, was that we should interview one or two members of the Residents' Action Group outside their homes with this awful convoy grinding slowly along behind them. Things got off to a bad start because the traffic was so bad we were half-an-hour

126

late arriving. Then, when we finally parked the cars, members of the group insisted we have coffee with them. Mike agreed this was a good idea but before he'd even finished the cup he was off exploring the house for a loo.

Eventually we got everyone outside and set up the camera. Just as we were about to start recording the first interview I noticed that the heavy, life-wrecking, misery-making traffic had suddenly, mysteriously disappeared. The odd lorry and car trundled merrily past, it was true, but there was certainly no congestion and if filmed like this it would make a mockery of the story.

Mike and I looked at each other and shrugged. This was Sod's Law. Over the months I had come to accept that whenever we produced a camera to film something doing something, that something stopped doing something and started doing something else. It was simply an occupational hazard.

Mike pottered off and started ripping up grass while the rest of us stood around chatting and telling jokes, waiting for things to deteriorate sufficiently for us to begin filming. Nothing happened. What little traffic there was about continued to zoom along quite freely and I started to panic.

Then one of the Residents' Action Group yanked on my sleeve and said: 'Here, g'vnor, if I was to break down in my car in the middle of the road down at the bottom of the hill there'd soon be a traffic jam, wouldn't there, and you can film your interviews?'

'That's true,' I admitted, and before I had a chance to say another word the fellow had said 'Righto, g'vnor' and was off to find his car.

I wasn't ecstatic about the arrangement but there seemed nothing I could do to stop him, and sure enough, a few minutes later a thin queue of cars and lorries began to form back up the hill. I called Mike back and together we knocked off the interviews pronto before the traffic evaporated once more.

What I hadn't realised was that one of the Residents' Action Group was a prospective local council candidate and, having watched what had happened, seized the opportunity for a little free publicity.

A few days later the local weekly newspaper carried a letter from the aforesaid prospective councillor, claiming that he had always

*The film that stopped the traffic.*

known the BBC rigged their documentaries and here at last was concrete evidence. He described, quite incorrectly, how a BBC employee had been instructed to break down in the road and how, quite incorrectly, this had given the wrong impression about the volume of traffic using the road. Nevertheless, the damage was done, and when I saw the letter I started leaping about like one of those European explorers from the Boy's Own Paper forced by African tribesmen to walk on hot coals. I prayed no one on the station would see the paper, and no one did; that is, until The *News of the World* picked up the story and made a meal of it.

'How is He this morning?' I asked Enid.

'Bit scratchy, I'm afraid,' she said. 'He's given up smoking again. Good luck.'

The Manager's office was the size of a small hangar. Somewhere on the other side of the room I could see Him scribbling away at his desk, and I crept in like a naughty boy summoned before the beak.

The BBC still has a system whereby every member of staff has an Annual Report, usually written by his Manager or Head of Department. Once a year the victim is allowed to read what has been written about him, viz. 'Farrell continues to make poor progress in his film-editing class . . .' or 'Farrell continues to be a pest to the junior members of staff . . .' and, being frightfully democratic, if he objects to the wording of his report, his objections must be recorded. The trouble is, of course, that you don't get to see the wording of the objection, so it probably reads something like: 'Naturally, Farrell objects to the true and fair remarks I have made about him, but then what would you expect from such a miserable little toad . . .' Either way, the Manager is an important person, and should not be crossed.

'Sit down,' said a distant voice from somewhere on the horizon, and as I gradually drew closer I realised He was smiling. Strange. For one wild moment I thought He may be about to congratulate me on using my initiative during the traffic incident.

He held up a copy of the *News of the World*.

'Have you seen this?' He asked, still smiling.

I told him I had and explained the circumstances. He listened attentively. When I had finished He slowly leant over His desk, took a deep breath and bellowed: 'If this ever happens again, you silly little beetle, I'll fire you!'

He gave me such a shock that I leapt a few inches in the air and nearly fell over backwards.

'Now — *get out*!'

The sequence was dropped from the film and I made up my mind never to let anything like it happen again.

The most difficult decisions we had to make on location, however, involved the handling of human distress.

Tragedy has always held a morbid fascination and, as television is able to depict it so powerfully, television journalists are particularly susceptible to exploiting it. I thought our standards were pretty high, but I was constantly surprised by the hostility shown by many people to the way we covered terrible incidents like train crashes or bomb blasts, murders, or the results of illnesses or disease.

The most common criticism, of course, involved interviewing the bereaved.

Don called me at home very early one morning and told me to set off at once to cover the murder of a young teenage girl whose body had been found beside a lonely stretch of canal.

The only way of covering big crime stories like this is to work in very close liaison with the police. So the day started with an early morning news conference, called by senior detectives anxious for as much publicity as possible in the hope that members of the public would come forward with clues.

Along with the familiar faces of local reporters and television crews assembling at the police station in the cold, frosty-clear early morning light were a large number of staff reporters from Fleet Street. It was a quiet news day and the murder was attracting a lot of attention.

We all stood around forcing down mugs of revolting police coffee, and then we were each given a photograph of the dead girl, reproduced from a snapshot from the family album, and a map showing the exact location of the attack. Two constables carried a table and two or three chairs into the room, and a hush descended as the Detective Superintendent, in charge of the murder enquiry, walked in. He gave a short resumé, along with a description of a car that had been seen in the area and an appeal to any walkers using the path beside the canal to come forward.

'Can we talk to the family?' someone asked.

The policemen consulted each other in whispers.

'We are not offering the family for interview,' said the senior detective at length. 'Not yet.'

Now, this was ambiguous. Whilst the police had no direct control over what we could, or could not do, a specific request to leave the family alone would have been honoured. Nobody enjoyed interviewing the bereaved; but many editors expected their reporters to try, some because they genuinely believed such interviews were a vital part of covering a story properly, others because they knew that any extreme of human emotion, be it happiness, anger or despair, made compulsive televsion. A definite statement by police that, in their opinion, there should be no interviews was a perfectly legitimate excuse for any reporter to offer his editor.

In this case there was no such statement.

The police are well aware of the value of such interviews. Providing it is felt the family is up to the ordeal, the police will often persuade the bereaved to talk to journalists because they know this will guarantee the story more prominence, more airtime. The logic is perfectly sound: the more the public's attention can be focused on the story, the better the chance of information coming forward.

We all trooped outside and one by one the radio and television reporters recorded an interview with the detective in charge. Then, in a long convoy, we followed a police car out to the scene of the murder. Here, teams of policemen were supposed to be busy combing the woodland around the spot where the body had been found, but in fact they were all in mournful little groups when we arrived, drinking tea from great aluminium urns. They were swiftly put back to work so that we could film them.

For half-an-hour we wandered about the scene of the tragedy, taking shots of the canal, shimmering in the chilly sunlight; it should have been a place of beauty, with great willow trees hanging down, dipping the tips of their branches into the water streaming past. It was difficult to believe that here, in the tranquility, a young girl had been pulled from her bicycle, raped and murdered just a few hours before.

After a time the reporters got together and decided that there should be an approach to the dead girl's parents but that it wouldn't be pressed if the answer was no. One of the Fleet Street men offered to put forward the request, and it was decided that if they agreed to talk a single interview for all the film crews would be recorded instead of expecting the family to go through the same thing half-a-dozen times. Like the advanced motorised column of a small army, the long convoy set off.

I think we all gave a small, secret sigh of relief when, our mighty cavalcade having completely blocked the cul-de-sac outside the family's house, our appointed representative knocked on the front door to discover there was no one at home. That was good enough. With everyone looking at their watches and mumbling about time, we said goodbye until the next time and one by one went our separate ways.

It was still early in the morning so we went for breakfast. We found a café where Ron knew the manager; Ron liked big breakfasts and I watched in silent admiration as he worked his way through a mountain of eggs, bacon, tomato, fried bread, mushrooms, kidney, sausages, baked beans and chips, specially prepared by the cook. The murder seemed more unreal than ever.

Just as we were leaving to return to the Bunker, a thought struck me. I said to Ron: 'Let's call in again at the house and see if the family are back.'

This time they were at home. It took a long time for the door to be opened, and when finally it did I was shocked by the look of drained despair on the face of the dead girl's father. He was struggling to control himself. I realised immediately I had made a mistake by calling; but it was too late.

I explained who I was, and apologised.

He looked at me silently for a long time. Suddenly he no longer seemed distraught, but genuinely puzzled.

'What on earth do you expect me to say?'

I said: 'Look, it could make the difference between this story appearing on local television or national television, that's all.'

There was another long pause. I felt I had to keep talking. 'The police want as much publicity as possible for this case. It could reveal a vital clue.'

At last he spoke again. 'I'm going to ring the police now, and if they agree with what you have just told me, then I will give you an interview.'

We stood around awkwardly in the front garden while he disappeared inside. I could hear his voice, deep and resonant, from somewhere in the house. We shouldn't have been there; but I was

132

happier now that he was talking to the police. They would justify my actions.

A few moments later he reappeared. A chill ran down my back. He looked drained again, cheated.

'They say I shouldn't talk to you.'

For a moment I was so surprised I didn't say anything. I couldn't believe the police had let me down so badly.

The man stared at me blankly. Was there no contempt in his eyes?

There was nothing to be done. I apologised, nodded to Ron and together we began walking back down the street.

Strangely, our obvious deflation seemed to change his mind. He called us back, said 'What do you want to know?' and there and then we filmed a short, sad and very moving interview.

When I told Don what had happened, he was furious. He immediately telephoned the police and demanded an explanation. He was passed from one detective to another but couldn't trace the policeman who had actually given the advice to the dead girl's father. Eventually he picked up the gist of police policy; they were hoping to hold back an interview with the girl's family until later in the week.

'That way they keep the story bubbling away in the local media,' Don explained. 'Instead of putting all their eggs in one basket. Next Friday, say, they'll organise a news conference and we'll all be leading our bulletins with: 'Today for the first time the parents of the murdered girl ...' Shouldn't have done that to you, though.'

That same night my interview appeared on all the national television news bulletins throughout the evening. As a result, a flood of information about the murder poured into the local police station.

Much later the Falklands War brought the whole subject of interviewing the bereaved back into debate. The home front was right on our doorstep; we filmed every British ship leaving Southampton and Portsmouth and we filmed those that survived when they returned. As in the old days when I wrote the obits. for the local paper, I found the subject of death divided the world into two groups: those who refused to discuss it and those who refused to discuss little else.

133

The war in the South Atlantic produce some extraordinary examples. One woman whose young son had been killed in the Exocet attack on HMS *Sheffield* suffered an appalling series of mistakes in information on his death. At first she was told that her son, a cook on board, had been killed; then she was told that this report was wrong, and that he had in fact survived the attack; then came the definitive news that he had indeed perished.

In the office we were all surprised to hear that the woman actually wanted to be interviewed. Don asked for volunteers and Jenni bravely said she'd go.

A few hours later she returned in buoyant mood.

'She was magnificent, quite magnificent. She sparkled with pride at what her son had done and been through,' she said, almost bouncing with excitement and enthusiasm. 'She really wanted everyone to know.'

It was a pattern which repeated itself time and time again. Many families contacted us direct asking for their dead sons, or husbands, or brothers, or fathers to be remembered; each night there were angry 'phone calls from the bereaved demanding to know why the names of their loved ones had not been included.

•　　•　　•

The repercussions of the appalling pig-biting incident continued unabated. From now on there was to be no argument in the office about who was to cover any animal stories: the universal cry was 'Send Farrell!' and I knew darned well that everyone was secretly hoping I would return from each mission covered from head to toe in teethmarks and with hundreds of feet of side-splitting film.

For a while, funny things did keep happening. I tried to interview a man holding a gigantic white cockatoo on his arm. Every time he attempted to answer my first question the wretched bird went berserk, screaming and squawking like an avian demon. We persevered, take after take; but no sooner did our man draw breath to speak than the bird was off again, deafening Tim so much that the poor chap had to rip off his recording headphones like lightning for fear of suffering permanent hearing loss. By about Take 37 we were all hysterical, too; and when at last we got our break and the animal shut up for a few seconds the shot was useless because the camera on Mike's shoulder was going up and down, up and down, as he fought to control his silent, mounting laughter.

*More animal magic.*

When Don saw the out-takes he nearly wet himself, and we slipped into a familiar formula, viz: 'Hey Jenni, come and see this, funniest film ever . . .'; Farrell was ignored, hoots of laughter came from the corridor, it had pride of place on the programme, viewers loved it, etc., etc. And every time, the pig-biting incident was hauled out from the film library and shown yet again.

After the cockatoo, there was the boa constrictor. This disappeared down the fellow's trousers mid-interview and we had to abandon filming whilst the trousers were removed and snake located. Of course, Mike actually kept the filming, so it was 'Hey, Jenni, come and see this . . .' Then I was in the middle of a deadly serious interview about hunting when the horse being held by my interviewee suddenly took an unnatural interest in my tie and tried to remove it whilst I was tackling the fellow with a penetrating, highly intelligent question; 'Hey, Jenni, come and see this . . .' etc., etc.

Slowly, however, the incidents became less and less funny until one day Don sent me out to make a film about a three-legged donkey condemned to the knacker's yard and seemed disappointed when I returned and told him nothing funny had happened at all.

'Rubbish, Nige, you're just being modest, hand over the film,' said Don, chuckling with anticipation and rushing off to the film editor's suite to study it. He returned several minutes later and, without a word, handed back the film and shuffled away, dejected.

I felt I had let him down.

In between these idiotic animal episodes I had started to do much more work in the studio: live news reports, interviews and, more and more, presenting the programme with Bruce or Jenni.

Presenting the show was a nerve-wracking, exhilarating way of earning a living. The pace of the day was in inverse proportion to that of the rest of the world: it began at a leisurely walk mid-morning; by lunch time it had broken into a jog; by mid-afternoon we were all running to keep up with events; and by 6 p.m., with Don's pile of cartoons at its peak, and when most sensible folk are on their way home from work, adrenalin levels were smashing all known records.

The key to success in the studio lay in the hands of the floor-manager. He, or she, was nominally in charge of everything on the studio floor; armed with a small microphone pinned onto a shirt or jumper and a pair of headphones. The floor-manager was the direct link between presenters, reporters, scene-shifters and studio cameramen, and the battery of technicians led by the programme director, who sat in front of a bank of television screens, in a little room adjacent to the studio called the gallery. The programme was controlled from the gallery; from here the director, barking out instructions, would select his shots from the four studio cameramen; the sound engineer could monitor the studio microphones and the lighting man could control his lights. Behind the director sat Don, hunched away in the shadows, smoking like a small blast-furnace and madly etching away on scrap paper as the programme progressed.

Just after lunch each day everyone involved with the programme would assemble, amidst the chaos of the newsroom, to hear Don announce his provisional running order for the items due in that evening's programme. It tended to be a little anarchic, with Don pacing up and down the room in a small, grey cloud of smoke, trying to maintain control amidst a barrage of cheeky schoolboy comments. After 20 minutes we would generally all be so confused that Don would turn to Enid, the only person in the room who had kept a record of what he had said, for the definitive schedule.

One afternoon an argument between Bruce and Don about the monotonous regularity with which a local football manager had been appearing on our programme was in full flood when in walked a very tall girl with beautiful, long, dark hair and a pretty, sad face. She had big, wide eyes which darted nervously from Bruce to Don as they spoke. When the meeting broke up in total disarray the girl looked lost for a moment until she was scooped up by Enid who began introducing her around the room. I watched, amused, as they made their way to where I was sitting; Enid was chattering away to several different people at once and the girl didn't seem to understand a word of what was being said.

'Yes, of course, Don, we'll try to get a line to London immediately. Yes, I know Bill said they're all booked. Ah! Nigel! meet Sam, our new floor-manager. But Brian, the Post Office won't release another line ...'

I looked at the girl and smiled. She was very attractive; the studio looked like being a brighter place.

'How do you do?'

The girl smiled back and we shook hands politely. Then she took a deep breath, and said slowly: 'Vot do you do herr?'

At first I thought she was joking; but as she stood there with the fixed, polite smile of a foreigner, the ghastly truth began to sink in.

Appointing a floor-manager who wasn't fluent in English was like sentencing everyone in the studio to perpetual pandemonium. The consequences were too awful to contemplate.

For the first few days Sam shadowed our regular floor-manager, Liz, whose calm and reassuring manner we had all come to take for granted. Bruce and I were presenting the show for the week and as Liz flitted silently around the studio giving us our cues with perfect efficiency, we watched the beautiful Sam crash around behind her like a great elephant, tripping over cables and walking into cameras. We felt a growing sense of despondency.

Sam was so appalling that her planned solo debut was postponed on Liz's insistence and we all tried to give her a quick course in basic English. She was such a lovely, sweet-natured girl that it was impossible to get cross with her; but eventually, we knew and she knew, she would have to manage alone.

The bulk of our programme consisted of film inserts, each played in from the big telecine machine which required a 10 second run-up to reach its proper speed. The introduction to each film was read live in the studio by the presenter, so 10 seconds before the presenter had finished his words, the director would instruct the telecine operator to run the film and the floor-manager would then count out the seconds, on her fingers, so that the presenter could end his words exactly as the film reached speed.

If you think that sounds complicated, try explaining it to a young German girl who doesn't speak proper English and you'll begin to see the problem.

Normally, our little studio was a quiet, ordered, *sensible* place. Most of it was in darkness; but the lights hanging in rows from the ceiling were positioned so that at the flick of a switch any part of it could be plunged into a pool of light — the two presenters, seated at desks, side by side; the interview set, with two hideous 'comfortable' chairs that were the most uncomfortable I've ever had the misfortune to sit on; the weatherman and his spinning map. In between, the cameramen, still studying their pornographic magazines in silent concentration, would push their big cameras about from one position to another like automatons. In the corner, at a shadowy desk, sat Janet, the teleprompt lady, running her thin paper script through a machine which magnified it and threw the words onto the lens of the presenter's camera.

It was slightly eerie, unnatural place, but it operated with reliable competence providing the floor-manager kept everyone aware of precisely what was happening.

Sam's first programme was purgatory. Every time she received an instruction from the director via her headphones, she shouted down into her little microphone in a stage-whisper: 'Vot vas that, again pliss?' Often, there was no time to repeat the instruction, and so all kinds of things would suddenly start happening around Sam and, in despair, she would go rigid, like a statue, and that fixed, empty smile would freeze across her pretty face. Last-minute changes in the running-order went unheeded; props were knocked over; maps and photographs dropped off their mounts; cues were non-existent. Every time Sam tried to count me down into a film her finger movements were so feeble and unsure that it would have been madness to rely on them; they would usually stop at a vital moment, about six seconds in, as Sam had second thoughts about whether she was right, and I was left totally at sea either way, with no idea whether a film was about to appear, and if so, when. Sam would just freeze again, and that awful, expressionless smile would stare back at me blankly.

Bruce was furious; not so much with the girl herself, but with a system which put her in the job at all. Fortunately, Bruce always used an earpiece so that he could hear the director's every word — something most presenters find too distracting — and he was able to battle masterfully on through the turmoil.

Don required stretcher-treatment and in the post-mortem he looked near to blowing a fuse.

'Vos I all right, OK?' asked Sam afterwards and we all looked at each other like desperate men, wondering how to make a start.

Over the days Sam plodded on blindly, but unlike most learners her performance appeared to deteriorate with practice. We put our minds to finding a way of doing without a floor-manager; Don gradually became a jibbering wreck.

Don asked me to present the programme on my own during the Easter holiday, and for days beforehand the image of Sam's fixed smile haunted me like a ghastly spectre. The final item in the show was to be a special Easter forecast from our weatherman, Keith, and the idea was that when he'd finished his bulletin I would walk into shot, thank him, turn to camera, wish all our viewers a happy Easter, and say goodnight. A short, specially shot film sequence of the bells of a local cathedral in action would then end the programme and we would 'opt' back into the network.

Most of it went much better than I had dared expect. Don had made sure the programme was a simple assembly and, as there was little news about over the holiday, he, the director and I had plenty of time to prepare our running-order and as far as possible make sure it was Sam-proof.

139

We negotiated the introduction into the final film successfully, and whilst this was being transmitted I asked Sam to tell me exactly how long we had before we joined the national network programme. From this I could work out how much time Keith had for his weather forecast and I for my final goodbyes.

Sam asked the director for accurate timings, and I heard her say: 'Vot vas that, again pliss?' four times. 'Sam, please,' I pleaded. 'The film's nearly finished . . .'

There was another pause, Sam bellowed: *'Vot vos that, pliss?'* again and suddenly the film was over and we were live once more.

I forced myself to smile and introduced Keith. As he began his forecast I tiptoed over to Sam and tried to take over her headphones so I could get the time-check myself, but as I was struggling with her I heard Keith winding up.

Smoothing down my hair I stepped into shot, thanked him, and turned to camera. I hadn't the slightest idea how long I should talk for, and as I began staring into the black camera lens inanely I noticed with horror that the frightful smile had fixed itself across Sam's face.

I took a deep breath and inadvertently embarked on the longest sentence I have ever spoken in my life.

I had decided I had no choice but to wind up the programme and just hope I had hit on the right timing by luck, so the sentence began with something banal, like:

> Well, that's it from us this Easter, and on behalf of Keith and all his noble workers at the Met. Office, as well as all of us here . . .

I was poised to finish with: ' . . . a very happy Easter . . . ' when I suddenly noticed that Sam's fixed smile had become a feverish grin. She was nodding her head triumphantly and waving one finger about in the air. A one-finger signal meant that there was in fact one whole minute before we were due to opt back to the network; one whole minute that may just as well have been one whole hour.

Try holding your breath for a minute and you'll see what I mean.

So instead of saying ' . . . a very happy Easter . . . ' I launched into a list of all those people in the studio who, I felt sure, would like to wish our viewers a Happy Easter.

Well that's it from us this Easter, and on behalf of Keith and all
his noble workers at the Met. Office as well as all of us here . . .
er . . . um . . . er . . . the er people without er whom this
programme would never um get on air . . . um . . . um . . .
the secretaries, the sub-editors, the film editors, the film
cameramen . . . er . . . um indeed, the studio cameramen,
mustn't leave them out, ha! ha! . . . the lighting men, the
graphics staff . . .

I blundered on. The monologue got a little out of control, its
phrases and sub-phrases taking over so that I had forgotten how the
sentence had started.

. . . the sound recordists, the set designer and his gracious
assistant, the ladies in the canteen, God bless 'em . . .

Still an agonising 15 seconds to go, according to Sam's frenetic
gesticulations . . .

. . . the receptionist, the security man on the door . . . the
cleaners

At last, Sam started waving her fingers about spasmodically, which I
took to be the start of the 10-second count-out, and I struggled
desperately to remember how this appalling sentence had started so
I could draw it to a close with some semblance of dignity. Mercifully
the point of it all came back in a flash . . .

. . . yes, from us all, a very, very Happy Easter!

I walked out of the studio, mopping my brow as if emerging from
a Turkish bath. Don appeared from the gallery. His face, too, looked
very hot and his eyes had a wild look about them.
'Sorry, Don.'
'She's got to go,' he managed to say at last. He dragged in on his
cigarette and stared blankly at the ceiling. 'And what's more, you
didn't even mention the bloody Manager!'
From behind us that frightful voice piped up again.
'Vishing you arl a 'appy Heaster!' it chirped merrily.
'Happy Easter, Sam,' we both replied, in unison.
More frequent appearances in the studio, coupled with the
constant repetition of the pig-biting incident, meant my face became

more and more recognisable to the public. People in shops and in the street would come up and poke me in the ribs to see if I was real; a variety of strange mail arrived on my desk, ranging from a retired Lieutenant-Colonel who described me as a 'bespectacled bastard fit only to rot in hell' to a 16-year-old schoolgirl who suggested I pay her a visit between 2-4 p.m. any second Friday in the month, when she could guarantee her parents would be out and their double bed available.

I received a few invitations to open local fêtes and carnivals — Bruce and Jenni received hundreds a year — but I turned these down whenever possible. In a wild moment I accepted a speaking engagement for a one-parent club, which I assumed would be full of young, attractive divorcees but which turned out to consist of six OAPs, two of whom fell fast asleep within minutes of me opening my mouth. Their snores drowned most of what I had to say anyway.

Many of our extra-curricula activities ended up being rather like work, particularly when in public we were expected to perform. Bruce got us organised for a cricket match against Terry Wogan's XI from London and, thanks mainly to T. Wogan's presence, a massive crowd turned out.

It was with a certain feeling of trepidation and after a very good lunch, liberally washed down with vats of excellent wine, that I found myself at the crease for the first time in 15 years. Mr Wogan was bowling and took a very long run-up indeed, coming into the wicket at the speed of Bob Willis. His delivery, however, was one of the slowest and most inaccurate in the history of the game. As it wobbled down pathetically about a mile to my left, I stepped out, took a wild slash at it, and miraculously hit a six. Even more surprisingly, I did exactly the same thing on the next ball.

As I was waiting for the third delivery, I felt, with growing alarm, that the plastic box carefully positioned in my underpants to protect my vital organs from the ravages of the cricket ball (I should have had one of those for Pinky) had begun to slip. Working with a mind of its own, it dropped slowly down my thigh and came to rest on my left knee, as though I had a large, fat mouse strolling down my trousers. This would have been an ideal arrangement for anyone with sensitive knee-caps but if Mr Wogan chose this for an accurate ball my family tree could have come to an abrupt and painful end.

*Like a pink blancmange . . .*

In fact, the next ball was miles from the stumps, and once again I stepped out to slog it; this time, however, I edged the ball and it ran on to the wicket.

Now I had to face the long, long walk back to the pavilion. My pads were very loosely strapped up, so in order to prevent the box slipping still further I was forced to bend my left leg to keep my trousers taut and, leaning forward to keep my balance, I began to hobble forward in short, spastic movements.

This strange, lopsided gait not only gave me the appearance of a crab but made very slow progress indeed. It seemed to take a decade to approach the boundary; the ground fell into a hush, as though I was about to perform some dramatic or religious act, and I felt a thousand pairs of eyes on my back.

Then, just as I thought I had made it, I straightened my leg an inch or two to ease the growing cramp and with a small plop! the box emerged from my trouser leg and sat on the grass like a pink blancmange for all to admire.

Accompanied by a deafening cheer from the crowd, I grabbed it and ran.

143

# 10

With the coming of a long, glowing summer, life on the road became easier, more relaxed, more civilized. Gone were the hours stamping about in the freezing darkness of early morning, interviewing striking dockers, or huddled over the geriatric heater in Mike's old van, waiting to film farmers digging out their sheep from the snowstorms whipped inland from the Channel's south-westerly gales. We could film from dawn (at four a.m.) to dusk (at nine p.m.) and with the rich colours of the sea and countryside brought alive by the sun, day after day, the batteries of lights all the cameramen carried with them lay unused and cobwebbed in their big black boxes.

I had never known so much fresh air. I covered sailing at Cowes, racing at Goodwood and Navy Days at Portsmouth. There were marathons, hours of village cricket and strawberry picking. There were the agricultural shows, always the same, year in, year out; sometimes it rained a little, sometimes it didn't, nobody cared much, the shows never changed, whatever the weather. I'd arrive early, send off the crew to shoot anything pretty which caught their eye, have a few tipples with half-a-dozen stallholders, film their stalls, and after a few more tipples, finish with the obligatory interview with the show organiser, who would blather on for a minute or two about how the attendance had dropped slightly/increased slightly since last year. Oh, then a final farewell tipple or two before departure. Very civilized.

There were hot-air balloon races, gliding championships, hunting and local boat shows. The latter became an annual summer carnival because London would normally loan us an outside broadcast unit and we'd transmit the whole programme live from the show. Afterwards, the entire station would be invited for drinks in the press office. At nightfall there'd be dancing amongst the boats, and people whom you thought hated each other ended up going home together. That glorious summer provided the most memorable boat show knees-up for years: the press office was one of those portable

*The joys of summer on the road.*

office cabins that was stacked above another, rather like the upper half of a bunk-bed. So many people arrived at the same moment that just as the pints of G and Ts were being dished out the floor gave way and half the staff disappeared from view. Some of the press people standing by the safety of the walls were so far gone that they didn't realise what had happened and stepped out blindly into the abyss; others had to hang on for dear life until rescued, whilst 'the disappeared' eventually reached ground level and made their own way home, bruised and bleeding, like Napoleon's army retreating from Moscow.

At lunch times Bruce, Jenni and I would often wander down to one of the waterside bars and sip orange juice or lemonade and watch the huge, flat-nosed container ships stagger up-river in the baking mid-day sun. In the evenings we would sweat away in our windless little black box of a studio and wonder, with the world out there playing in the evening sun, if anybody was really watching.

The summer was a good time for everyone except Don. Finding enough material to fill the programme every day in a normal week could be difficult enough; in high summer it often became a nightmare. Parliament and local councils were in recess. Courts, schools, factories were closed. Everyone, including those vital ingredients to any self-respecting news programmes, the bank robbers, rapists and murderers, seemed to be on holiday. This was the silly season, and whilst most of us slowed down a little in the sunshine, poor Don would pace up and down the corridors in anguish lest he end the day with an empty programme. Occasionally, odd little noises of panic would escape from him as he strode up and down, up and down - an inane giggle here, a sharp yelp there as he absentmindedly let the cigarette he was holding burn down to his fingertips.

On bad days there was an air of great tension among those unfortunate enough to be chained to the office. The newsroom journalists would sit around trying to look busy. Every telephone call was jumped on immediately, in the hope that it bore some horrific news story that would save the day. They took it in turns to sit on the forward planning desk and set up items to fill future programmes, so during slack periods those in the hot seat could then be roundly criticised by the others for failing in their duty. This constant threat to the peaceful running of the newsroom was removed one day when it was simply announced that the forward planning desk had been abolished. Thereafter no one was to blame for empty programmes.

During the silly season it was well for a reporter to make himself scarce. This was a time when, in desperation, we were sent out on those really daft stories that at any other time wouldn't get a look in. It was at moments like these that Don would hover outside the gentlemen's lavatory in the hope of nabbing me emerging from a good hour's study of the morning papers. 'Research, Don,' I'd explain, before being immediately dispatched on some godforsaken mission. Sometimes one hid in the canteen, or the bar; checking library material in a distant film editing suite was always a good ruse, as was a visit to Menita, on the floor above, to check expenses. With any luck, Don would corner one of the other reporters first; but if he finally caught up with you, you could see him fighting to restrain himself from reaching out and twisting off your ear, like a beadle with a naughty Victorian street-urchin. In my case, there was usually some particularly idiotic animal story in store; interviewing a pipe-smoking parrot perhaps, or a sheep undergoing psychiatric treatment for thinking it was a horse.

There was one dreadful old chestnut, however, which was always a last resort when the programme needed filling at short notice, and even now the memory of it fills me with gloom.

The late 1970s produced one of the longest-running international news stories since the Second World War. Under threat of constant persecution from their own government, hundreds of thousands of middle-class Vietnamese decided to flee their own country and seek sanctuary overseas. Many, bearing little more than the clothes on their backs, put to sea in overcrowded little fishing boats, and simply prayed for deliverance. Thousands drowned or starved; but some survived because, by chance, they were picked up by passing, sympathetic ships, many of them European, British among them, which took their pitiful cargoes straight to Hong Kong. From there, hundreds were flown to Britain where a number of camps were set up to rehabilitate them and prepare them for our society.

The first such camp was a converted RAF base at the little village of Sopley, in Hampshire. It was a perfect story for local television, and over those first few weeks Mike or Ron's camera was always near to record the constant stream of arrivals, and the first timid steps that these people from the other side of the world were taking into their new, very English way of life.

At first, it was all fascinating stuff. The images of the camp had a curiously intriguing quality about them; the monotonous grey concrete of the RAF living quarters suddenly brought to life by endless criss-crossed lines of brightly-coloured washing flapping gently in the wind; the old guardroom and administrative blocks that were almost hidden behind a sea of newly-painted signs, in English and, of course, Vietnamese; and above all, the small, beautiful and always slightly puzzled Oriental faces of the refugees themselves, which moved against a backdrop not of jungle or paddy-fields but of the gentle green woodlands, the fields of leaning corn and overgrown hedgerows of rural Hampshire.

The trouble was that we tended to overdo it, as with most of the best stories. There is a reluctance in television to let a good story die. Instead of following the reliable and proven formula of leaving the audience wanting more, desperation sometimes pushes the story until it is flogged to death. Then it's even squeezed a bit more.

I reported on the very first Vietnamese refugees to come to

147

Sopley, and on the second and third groups a few days later. I went back there after a month, and again after two months. I made films about the start of English classes at the camp, woodwork classes, needlework classes; then I made a follow-up series of films on how these classes were progressing. I made a film about how the refugees were upsetting some of the local people and another on how some of the local people were upsetting the refugees. I made a film on how the Vietnamese eat, and another on how they were being retrained for the outside world. I made a film about the progress of the camp after six months, another after a year, another after two years. Then I reported on how the camp was due to close in six months time, and another six months later on why it hadn't closed in six months time. In short I made so many darned films at Sopley that after a time I used to study my face in the bathroom mirror in the belief that I was actually beginning to look Vietnamese.

Every time I was asked to make yet another film there my protests were dismissed with the devious, age-old BBC argument that I had now become something of an expert on the subject and was therefore the best person for the job.

I arrived for work one sunny morning, with the prospect of a lazy day ahead catching up on my expenses and sipping an icy drink for lunch down by the river, when I was spotted by Enid, steaming down the corridor with one of the newsroom typists in tow.

'— anyway, I said to Bob, ''Was that the best thing to say, given the appalling mess Terry had got himself into?'' — Ah! Nigel, my sweet, hang on a moment! — and Bob said he didn't think Terry knew what he was talking about —.'

'Yes, Enid?'

'Ah, Nigel, did you know that Don is looking for you?'

I said I didn't, not for a moment liking the tone of her voice.

'I'm afraid it's Sopley again.'

A wave of despair swept over me at the mere mention of the place. 'I don't believe it!'

Enid smiled sympathetically.

Timidly, I pushed open the door of the reporters' room and peered inside. Bruce was already busy typing at his desk, but when he saw me he started to laugh.

'Have you seen Don?'

148

I put a finger to my lips, crept in, hid my briefcase behind a desk, and was just about to dash silently out when the newsroom hatch crashed open. Like a sniper, I dropped out of sight behind a chair.

'Any sign of that idiot Farrell yet?' I heard Don demand. 'Tell him I want to see him the moment he arrives.'

With the sound of the hatch being slammed shut, I gave Bruce a conspiratorial wink and shot out of the room, in the hope of making it to the sanctuary of the graphics department at the end of the corridor. I was poised to make it when Don's voice stopped me like a bullet in the back.

'Nige, thank goodness I've found you! Great little story for you, you'll love it, right up your street!'

'Don, I wanted to —.'

'Guess what? It's at Sopley, your favourite location!' Here Don allowed himself an evil little chuckle, before anxiety suddenly set his face to stone again. 'You'll have to move fast, London want this story as well. It's all about the Ying family and I won't give you all their names now because there are 172 of them.'

Ever since the camp at Sopley had opened, the authorities had been anxious to speed up the acclimitisation programme so that the Vietnamese could be found homes and jobs as quickly as possible. This wasn't always easy. With so many Vietnamese crowded together in one place, many did not find it necessary to learn English and of those that did, most had such trouble with the language that they couldn't hope to survive satisfactorily in the outside world. While dispersing the refugees across the country, the plan was to make sure families could stay together if they wished.

With one family this proved a particular problem. They were the Yings, a fishing family of no less than 172 members who, despite leaving Vietnam at different times, had miraculously all managed to become reunited at Sopley.

The story centred about what was to happen to the Yings now. One proposal put forward was that a disused monastery in the Highlands of Scotland should be offered them so that the whole family could remain intact.

Before long, the morning's filming was teetering on the edge of disaster.

Someone in the office had told me just before I'd left that several

149

of the Ying men had been passing their spare time making wooden spears, like those they had used for fishing in the seas around Vietnam. It had been arranged that we should take some of the men down to the sea, a few miles from the camp, and get some shots of the spears in use.

This sounded a bit ambitious but nevertheless, as I drove through the main gates and was greeted like an old friend by the aged, wizened Vietnamese lady who always stood guard, I resolved to give it a try. The other idea I had in mind — and later wished I hadn't — was to assemble all 172 memebers of the Ying family for a huge family photograph.

It took me half-an-hour to find the interpreter and half-an-hour for her to find half a dozen of the Ying fishermen. It took another half-an-hour for them to find the little spears they had made.

'The men are happy to stand holding their spears wherever you like for the photo,' the interpreter said obligingly, smiling broadly. I don't know why it is that interpreters always smile broadly, but smile broadly they invariably do. In this case I couldn't help but notice what a perfect set of teeth the girl possessed.

I explained that what was required was for the men to come down to the sea where we could film them actually spearing fish.

The interpreter translated this, and when she had finished the men suddenly burst out laughing. Then they slapped each other on the back and pointed at me as though what I had said was the funniest thing they had heard since leaving Vietnam.

The interpreter turned back to me, grinning like a Cheshire cat.

'This is not possible. You have not understood. The spears are not real fishing spears, but ceremonial spears, a decorative symbol only of their days at home.'

I cursed the office. The trouble with office staff was that they never had to face the practical nightmares of location filming.

The men had stopped laughing now and were waiting patiently to be told what to do. I put forward a proposal that, like so many on location, was borne from mounting panic.

'Could you ask the men if they would be prepared to come down to the sea anyway and try to fish with the spears so that at least we could have a few shots of them in action?'

This was relayed to the men and once again they burst out

*The Yings go fishing.*

laughing, slapping each other's backs harder still and pointing at me with such repeated vigour I was afraid that at any moment they might hurl their spears at *me* just for fun.

'The men say OK, they have nothing better to do and that it may be . . .' here she paused, searching for a phrase, '. . . it may be good for a laugh.'

I had imagined a comical scene at the seaside and I had been right. It was a sunny July day and the beach was brimming with jolly holiday-makers. There were fat men and their fat wives baking like lobsters on deckchairs and inflatable beds. There were cohorts of little children throwing sand and ice cream at one another; in the shade of a vast red umbrella an old man fought conspicuously to remove his wet trunks from beneath his towel.

Right in the middle of this uniquely British scene a group of brightly-dressed little Vietnamese men stood in the tiny breakers as

151

they lapped gently onto the pebbly sand, shrieking with merriment and hurling short shafts of wood all over the place.

It didn't, quite, work. With absolutely no danger of anyone getting anywhere near actually catching a fish, I considered dashing off to a local fishmongers and buying a couple of cod to stuff onto the end of the spears — a common ploy amongst film crews on fishing stories — but lack of time forced me to abandon the idea.

I arrived back at the camp exhausted.

'Is there anything else required?' asked the interpreter.

I had not got enough material for my film but looking at my watch I realised I could allow myself only ten more minutes at the camp.

'Look,' I said, 'Can we try to round up all the Ying family quickly and get them in a line on the football pitch so that we can take a photograph of them all? It would make a great picture.'

I wished, very strongly at that moment, that the interpreter would stop grinning, if only for a few seconds.

She didn't.

'Are you serious?'

I said I was. She said it was impossible because the Yings were spread all over the camp and, anyway, no one was quite sure who they were. I said we had to give it a try.

Reluctantly, the interpreter set off in one direction, I in the other.

'Excuse me, are you a Ying?' I asked every Vietnamese face I passed. Most of them just smiled back at me blankly. One man pointed inexplicably at the sky, another beckoned me to wait a moment while he dashed inside his hut and reappeared a moment later with a large red football which he began bouncing on his head. It was hopeless.

Eventually, I had no choice but to give up. I ran about the camp like a lunatic looking for the interpreter. When I found her I grabbed her arm wildly. This was not a moment to pontificate.

'Sod the Yings!' I yelled. 'Grab the first 172 Vietnamese people you come across and get them over to the football pitch pronto!'

I think we ended up with over 200 in the group shot — we didn't have time to count them — and to this day I've no idea how many of them were actually Yings. It didn't seem to matter. At the office everybody was happy; in London everybody was happy; and if the

Yings themselves saw the film being transmitted, I don't expect they would have minded. None of them would have understood a word of what was being said anyway.

• • •

The demands of the 'faceless ones' in London were becoming greater and greater. Every day, London-based programmes were wanting copies of our best and most interesting films. Television news was the biggest customer, followed by 'Nationwide' and 'Newsnight'; with national news bulletins becoming longer and more frequent, good film stories were at a premium and the regions were in a strong position to supply them. This was one of the great advantages BBC TV news had over ITN.

Time was often so short that having to prepare a brief version of a film for London, as well as a full four or five minute story for our own programme, tended to place our whole rickety system under great strain. Nevertheless, national news always took priority so we raced about, like rats which had inhaled vast quantities of pure oxygen, to keep the London producers happy.

Usually, I would be squatting down, like a sprint-runner at the start of a big race, waiting for the rolls of film to emerge from the processing lab. Once safely handed over, I would dash down to a film editor and begin checking my script against shots as he synchronised the pictures with the rolls of sound tape recorded on location. He would then slice out the shots I wanted and, using nothing more complicated than a cutting block and lots of sticky tape, he'd assemble the finished film.

My commentary, when not read out live on transmission, would then be dubbed onto the soundtrack, along with any other sounds required, like music or special effects. There were all mixed together in what in those days we laughingly called a dubbing suite. This disaster area consisted of an old recording studio with bits of decrepit machinery hanging off the walls, and reams of sheet music scattered all over the floor by an engineer who spent most of the working day hidden away studying the guitar. The other half of the suite was about three-quarters of a mile down the corridor where the dubbing mixer sat, desperately trying to work out how to mix the sounds on such archaic equipment. His cubicle was positively medieval and was connected to the recording studio by an intercom system that looked as though it had been designed by Leonardo da Vinci on an off day, and it was normally broken. If the dubbing mixer wanted to say something to me like: 'Move further away from the mic.', or 'How the bleedin' ajax does all this work, squire?' he would have to walk all the way down to me in the studio which, as he'd stop and chat to half-a-dozen of his mates en route, could take twenty minutes. The only other communication was the usual small green light on the studio-desk which the mixer would flash when he wanted to cue me to read my commentary.

The engineers regularly swapped jobs after a few months which complicated matters, so that just as one had begun to master the mysteries of the system he would be replaced by a complete novice who would be spellbound by its deficiencies. Then the appalling, beautiful Sam started to be seconded to 'help out' in the dubbing suite. We would sit around for several hours waiting for Sam to bring a vital sound effects record, only to discover she had forgotten all about it and had gone shopping instead.

Things came to a head when national news asked for a 45 second version of a film I had made about the rescue of the crew of a fishing boat which had caught fire in the Solent. One of the shots, which had been filmed mute, included a hovercraft passing close by the stricken vessel. Sam was longer than ever trying to find a sound effects record that included hovercraft noises, but eventually we discovered the wretched disc was missing so we used the speeded-up sound of a lawnmower instead.

By the time we were ready to have a stab at dubbing the piece the national news was already on air, but I knew that there was still time to play it up onto one of London's videotape machines and from there into the end of the bulletin. We tried several times to get the dub right, but on each occasion — in mid-stream — my little green light started to flash hysterically, the traditional 'abort' signal. Then the intercom belched loudly, and the light cued me again. I read the commentary badly and was about to say: 'Oh balls, Henry, we're going to have to do this farting thing again,' when a sixth sense told me to finish the piece as best I could.

Afterwards, the little green light didn't flash again and I sat there like a stuffed prune for several minutes. Finally Henry shuffled in whistling 'The Yellow Rose of Texas', and started pulling out wires from a panel on the wall.

'Henry, would you mind telling me what's happening?'

'What do you mean, squire?'

'Are we going to dub this in time, or not?'

An empty expression swept across his face, like a curtain.

'Dub it? Dub it, squire? You've just done it — live into the bulletin.'

It took a moment or two for the awful truth to permeate the brain tissues. Then I had it: I had just broadcast live to the nation *without realising it*. The words: 'Oh balls, Henry, we're going to have to do this farting thing again' rang round my head like the echo of a giant bell.

Working at remote control to the main newsroom in London was like being employed by Howard Hughes. Our films were either 'sent up the line' or, occasionally, driven half way to the capital by car and picked up by a dispatch rider. We never actually met the people who put the national television news bulletins together, a lack of liaison which sometimes led to curious little misunderstandings.

Don must have run out of half-baked animal stories because one afternoon he collared me hiding behind the fish tank in reception and told me to go and find some prostitutes. 'We've just heard that the local council are to debate a proposal to legalise brothels in the city,' he explained casually. 'Great story, they should have done it years ago. Make it good, London want it too.'

We waited until nightfall, and then Mike picked me up in his van and we set off, terrified, in search of prostitutes to interview in the notorious red-light area of the city. I decided that the chances of finding someone willing to talk were remote, whilst those of ending up in the gutter with a boot in the mouth were pretty high. What by day was a seedy, depressing area of crumbling little victorian terraced houses became a sinister, violent place by night, where bloody battles between pimps were commonplace and the shadowy streets echoed to the sound of anonymous footsteps and unexplained screams.

After ten minutes of circling the area wondering how on earth to begin we realised several other vehicles were doing exactly the same: prowlers on the lookout for cheap, streetside sex, I thought, and no doubt they thought the same of us. I felt hidden eyes constantly upon us, particularly since every few circuits Mike had to furtively pull up his van so that he could do what had to be done.

Eventually, I decided the time had come to take the plunge so I asked Mike to stop outside a promising-looking house with a very bright red light and a large plastic doll hanging in the window.

'Right, in we go lads.'

Mike and Tim looked at me in silent conspiracy. Then Mike said: 'You go in first, and we'll follow when she's agreed to talk.'

I thought this was pretty lousy considering I was in need of moral support, but perhaps the sight of *three* men approaching the house might have unfairly raised the hopes of the occupant. So I walked over to the front door alone, my heart drumming wildly.

The door was ajar, with the thin, dim shaft of red light falling onto the tarmac path outside. Did one ring the bell?

In the distance a baby cried.

Gingerly, I pushed open the door and peered in. There was a in small hallway, its carpet worn, its wallpaper stained and peeling. Two doors led from it. One opened onto an apparently empty, bare-boarded front room, glowing the ghostly red from the lamp at the window. I pushed open the other door as timidly as a church mouse and, taking a deep breath, popped my head around it.

For a moment all I could distinguish was a television in the corner of the room, its volume so low that scarcely a whisper came from it.

Then, opposite, I was slowly able to make out the figure of a very large woman pushed into a very small black dress. She was smoking a long cigarette and, in the shadows, the light from the television screen played upon her face like dancing black and white squares on a chessboard. She glanced up, quite unperturbed, saying nothing, as if I was an expected guest who's arrived very late. I, in turn, stared back at her, mesmerised.

After we had been staring at each other for some time I thought it might be a wise move to say something. How did one begin? Did she want to know my name?

Searching desperately for appropriate words, I'm afraid I made rather an unimpressive opening gambit.

'Howdi'.

Now, 'Howdi' is a word I do not much like. Actually, I dislike it intensely. In fact, I hate it. It is an expression favoured by middle-aged men on holiday in Torremolinos whose striped open-necked shirts are always unbuttoned down to the waist to reveal a cheap medallion entwined in their greying chest hairs. 'Howdi' is a word which comes naturally to them. I do not have greying chest hair; I have never been to Torremolinos and I cannot recall ever having used the word 'Howdi' before; nevertheless, out it had popped and now there it was, and I could do nothing about it.

The prostitute's big eyes opened still further when I spoke. She had a pale, puffy face with a very wide mouth. To my surprise she wore no make-up at all. Perhaps it was her day off.

'Howdi', she said.

She stood there, her arms supporting her back like a pregnant woman, a formidable figure with powerful legs bulging from the tight dress.

'I'd like to talk to you.'

'Yeah, love?' She blew out a long thin line of cigarette smoke. 'That's up to you.'

'No, no,' I protested, and hurriedly explained who I was and why I was there.

'You work on the television?' she asked suspiciously when I had finished, and those big eyes suddenly narrowed. She looked on the point of asking me to leave. Then, after eyeing me up and down for several more moments, the eyes suddenly widened again and began to sparkle with recognition.

'Hang on, love. Aren't you that fellow what had his knackers bitten by that pig?'

I nodded, with relief, and the prostitute started grinning and asking me about what had happened. I showed her the scars that Pinky's teeth had left on my fingers and, as she bent down to study them in the half-light, I realised with a warm glow that I had won her over.

Pinky owed me a good turn.

'How's business?' I asked eventually, not at all sure that this was a polite question. She didn't seem to mind.

'Not like it used to be, love, when the port was busy. When one

157

of those big battleships dropped anchor there used to be queues around the block.' Her face took on a dreamy quality here, before being jerked back to reality. 'Not now, though, not like it was.'

I asked her about the council's proposal to establish a brothel. She seemed genuinely horrified. 'None of the girls here would want it.

*The lost microphone.*

Kill trade, love. What man who doesn't want to be publicly identified is going to use a public brothel?'

This was great stuff, and seeing her so impassioned I decided this was the moment to ask for an interview. She agreed without hesitation.

I think Mike was so worried that he didn't even ask for the boy's room but just marched straight in with his lights and camera gear and had set up in a moment. Tim asked the prostitute if she'd mind if he dropped a microphone wire down the inside of her dress so that he could pin the mic. to her lapel. This was standard practice — most sound recordists have put their hands up the insides of more dresses than most men have dreamed about — but on this occasion I noticed that for the first time ever Tim was actually blushing with embarrassment. The dress was so tight that the end of the wire got lost somewhere 'twixt cleavage and thigh which caused much wriggling and giggling on her part and much hot-fingered embarrassment on his. Finally, we knocked off a very good interview and within a few minutes we were on our way home.

National television news used my report in its entirety, and I knew they were happy with it because it was high up in the bulletin. I had reason to be pleased; after all, getting an interview with a charming, articulate, uninhibited prostitute was quite a little scoop.

Shortly after transmission one of the telephones rang in the newsroom. It was London.

'I've got a message from the News Organiser for one of your reporters, Nigel Farrell.'

'It is he speaking,' I replied confidently, the prospect of praise and public acclaim for my outstanding work now imminent.

'Well,' said the voice, 'The News Organiser has asked me to tell you that the next time you do a report for us make sure you wear a bloody tie.'

At first, I wasn't sure I had heard the man correctly. Then, as his words sank in, I began to wonder if the prospect of one day working on a major network programme in London was really a bit beyond my reach.

It very nearly was.

# 11

There certainly wasn't any need to look for another job; a comfortable respectability had started to seep into my life. I had mastered many of the deeper mysteries of filming and, at the same time, like Bruce, Jenni and the other well-known faces from the programme, I was on a perch in local society and there I sat, preening myself, twittering sweetly, without a care in the world.

At first, there was a peculiar fascination in the stream of invitations to open fêtes, present prizes and host charity events, which followed me around from desk to desk. The organizers normally tried me when Bruce or Jenni had already turned them down, but it was still flattering, as well as odd, to be asked. I actually found the task of addressing real human beings quite an ordeal compared to addressing an inanimate object like a camera, and I always refused.

We were constantly invited to cocktail parties, luncheons and receptions; at first, too, it was quite entertaining to study the chief constables, managing directors and MP's sitting around me. My only real worry was of having too many glasses of El Supremo and letting the side down by telling filthy jokes, squeezing the bosom of somebody's wife, falling off a chair or being sick. Not that anyone would have minded too much; us chappies from the media were usually expected to behave oddly — all part of the mystique, you see, as I found on the occasion when I was invited to a fancy-dress party.

After much consideration I decided to go to the party dressed as a spaceman. This was a mistake. I covered myself from head to toe in silver paper which I bound carefully around each limb, including feet, hands and head. To prevent the wretched silver stuff from slipping off I was forced to walk around very stiffly, as though in a suit of armour, trying not to bend a muscle. I left my front door and set off down the pavement in search of the car but as my field of vision was severely limited I kept on bumping into lamp-posts and garden fences. I noticed a next-door neighbour approaching me, deep in conversation with a companion. Suddenly seeing the bumbling silver spectre advancing towards him, he said, in words that were familar: 'Don't be alarmed, Cyril, he works for the BBC, you know,' and continued his earnest discussion as I ricocheted off a brick wall and shot past him, like a robot with a blown fuse.

Of course, the more snugly entrenched one became, the more cold and unpleasant the prospect of digging oneself out and venturing off into pastures new. Filming assignments which had once kept me up all night with nervous anticipation now took on an easy familiarity; when dispatched to cover the annual choir competition or town crier championships, Don would ask: 'Remember how you did it last year?'

*'He works for the BBC, you know.'*

Yet, sandwiched between the diary regulars, there was still plenty of material to keep my interest alive and my conversation-value at dinner parties topped-up. Every day I was interviewing show people, from Edna Everidge to Tommy Trinder; sportsmen, from Ian Botham to Kevin Keegan; singers like the Three Degrees; scientists like Sir Christopher Cockerell, and politicians like Denis Healey and Margaret Thatcher.

Then Don offered me a really big opportunity: an interview with Princess Grace of Monaco, on one of her rare visits to Britain.

The Princess was in this country to give a poetry recital at the festival theatre at Chichester; the morning before her performance had been set aside for a news conference, during which the Princess had, unusually, agreed to answer direct questions from reporters.

'This is the big one, Nige,' Don had said, once again adding that ominous phrase: 'London want this one, too; TV *and* radio. Make sure she says something good.'

There must have been 100 reporters, photographers and camera crew assembled in the theatre foyer, chattering away like the members of an exclusive little club, comparing notes, bosses, pay, interviewees, and outrageously exaggerated stories about 'the last job we worked on together'. Just as on all the big stories we were all ostensibly very chummy, slapping each other on the back etc., but secretly casting furtive glances around us all the time, like radar, in case we were missing something important. At the back of everyone's mind is the knowledge that his performance will be judged on how well he fares in the face of competition from other journalists. If one reporter gets an interview, we all must; if nobody gets it, nobody has failed, like a pack of hounds with a fox.

So there we all were, slurping down as much sherry as we could without drawing undue attention to ourselves, when suddenly it appeared the end of the world had come.

At the precise moment of chaos, I was listening politely to an elderly, rather dignified old hack from a local newspaper, in the middle of a long explanation of how he managed to grow purple miniature cucumbers whilst a prisoner-of-war in Italy. One moment the dear old boy had a benign smile playing on his lips and a distant, contented look in his eyes; the next, he had almost completely disappeared in a stampede of newsmen. I remember quite clearly the agonised look on his face as he was borne along, wide-eyed, bewildered, in a sea of bodies.

Princess Grace had arrived. She appeared at the top of a flight of stairs, immaculately dressed, smiling serenely, and waited for a moment with perfect timing as the first of the motor cameras began to click away impatiently. Then, slowly, she descended the staircase, a curious, stunning combination of Hollywood glamour and regal poise and sophistication.

I looked around desperately for Mike and his camera and, at first, I couldn't see him anywhere. With rising panic I was just about to set off for the Gents to hound him out when I caught sight of him on the floor, wriggling forward like a baby seal, squeezing through all the legs to get his shot.

The Princess disappeared from view behind the seething, moving wall of reporters and photographers. I lost her completely, and again I felt the first tremors of panic. I should have been in the middle of the scrum, battling for that interview.

With the superhuman energy of a man who realised he was on the point of making the kind of mistake which could ruin his reputation, I threw myself at the rear of the human wall in an effort to break through. I bounced off, rather like a rubber ball on a piece of concrete, and had to watch helplessly as the heaving mass moved slowly across the room. For a brief moment, I caught sight of my aged newspaper colleague whose thoughts would now be very far from purple cucumbers, miniature or otherwise. He was facing in completely the wrong direction and, with his body supported almost horizontally and his thin legs twisted behind him like broken wood, his face was frozen into an expression of silent pain as he was carried helplessly along.

It seemed that the Princess was in danger of being trampled to death. They are not used to riots at the Chichester Festival Theatre and thus are not equipped with what was required, viz. batton-charges, shields and water cannon. Eventually, however, a team of theatre staff managed to peel away the bodies and pull the Princess to sanctuary behind a barracade of tables that had been set up for the news conference.

Slowly, order was restored. On one side of the tables the camera crews pushed and struggled for position, whilst rows of soundmen from behind shoved microphones across on long booms, right under the nose of the seated Princess. On either side of her sat members of her personal staff and the theatre management, trying to quieten down the rabble.

At last, a very tall man stood up and announced that the Princess would spend a few moments answering questions. This was my moment. Buried well behind the vanguard of the party, I piped up with my contribution and was half-way through it before realising that no one was hearing a word I was saying, least of all the Princess herself who was leaning forward, listening intently to someone else's question.

Each time there seemed to be a pause in the action I started hopping up and down shouting out my question, but I'm afraid I was so far away no one took the slightest notice of me — no one, that is, save a dumpy little girl, with short spikey hair and a spotty face, standing immediately in front of me, who hissed like an angry snake and said that if I didn't shut up she would do something unpleasant to my feet. Why she chose *my* feet I cannot say, but there we are, and I wasn't going to argue.

My total impotence in the question session wasn't necessarily a disaster — after all, on occasions like this there was no opportunity for individual interviews so one simply filmed whatever answers were given. I could see that Tim had managed to poke his microphone quite near the Princess' head so we weren't going to miss anything. No, the real problem was far more serious than that, and it took me a moment or two to realise what it was — probably because I was still half expecting a savage attack on my feet, even though I *had* shut up.

The real trouble, it slowly dawned on me, was that Princess Grace wasn't opening her mouth. Not a single word did she produce. She was merely nodding and smiling sweetly at the assembled company. Whenever a response had to be given, she simply leant across to a tall, thin aide sitting beside her, who looked like a beanpole, and whispered her answer, quite inaudibly. The beanpole then relayed this to the masses.

Now in the old days, when newspapers ruled supreme, this kind of approach was fine — the photographers got their snaps and the reporters their quotes. But the idea of using a third person like an

*Fall from Grace.*

interpreter, particularly one looking like a beanpole, was a catastrophe for radio and television coverage.

'Does the Princess have any plans for other appearances whilst in this country?' Whisper, whisper. 'No, the Princess has no plans for more appearances.'

'Does the Princess intend to ever make another film?' Whisper, whisper. 'No, the Princess has no plans for more filming.'

See what I mean?

After a few minutes of this I felt near to weeping. The prospect of explaining again to London that things had gone wrong did not appeal; what made it worse was that radio news was relying on a copy of my soundtrack for their bulletins, too.

I started to shout again in the forlorn hope of persuading the Princess to say even a few words herself, but just as I got started I felt a searing pain in my left foot. It was so intense that for a moment my sight became blurred and Princess Grace's edges went stretched and fuzzy, and though I was seeing her reflection in a distorting mirror. Then, eventually, came blessed relief as the spikey-haired reptile removed her stiletto heel and my foot began getting used to an indentation the size of a small oil well.

I was just about to reach out and strangle the girl when another stampede was suddenly under way and there was my old newspaper friend being carried helplessly past me at high speed. The news conference was over and, within seconds, Princess Grace was bustled away out of sight.

When I explained what had happened to Don he was surprisingly sympathetic and immediately got on the telephone to apologise to London. I knew that this would ultimately be another blot in the old copy-book, and that however understanding they appeared, the word would be in the London newsroom that next time Farrell was involved they'd send down their own reporter to make sure the job was done properly.

This was depressing. 'Getting noticed' by sending up a series of well-received films to London was probably the best way of being offered a job as a national television news reporter. Southampton had a high reputation for the quality of its news coverage and many well-known correspondents and reporters had stepped into the national limelight from there.

But did I really want to be a hard news reporter? Did I want to grow old rushing to Flizborough disasters or great train robberies, interviewing rice-growing peasants in Thailand, or chasing drug-peddlars in New York? Could I really see myself in one of the plum posts of economics or political correspondant? Could a man whose private parts had been ravaged by an insane pig ever be taken seriously as a presenter of 'Panorama'?

For several days after the Princess Grace fiasco I limped about Southern England with a swollen foot, making films about two feuding best-kept villages and a school lollipop-lady who claimed her prize pumpkin had been stolen by ruthless competitors, trying to decide whether I should pull out all the stops for London, or settle back into quiet contentment where I was.

Then the decision was made for me.

It came about because at the time Jenni was dating a nutritional expert whose sister's boyfriend's brother's best-mate's girlfriend was a teacher at a school where some of the children had recorded a Christmas song and issued it as a disc. Don had suggested the story of how the disc came to be released would make a good film, but the day before it was due to be shot Jenni caught 'flu and Don asked me to take over.

I listened to the record before setting out and had to fight back the nausea. It was one of those appalling songs released every Christmas in which a cohort of angelic, freckly, toothless little children sing about Santa leaving a present for the snowman grandpa had made in the garden, or some such manure.

Driving to the school, I decided the easiest way of filming the song was for the children, their scrubbed and shining little cherubs' faces beaming at the top of starched white shirts and blouses, to mime to the original soundtrack which we would play over a loudspeaker. Rather than have the little dears simply standing there like rows of polished bananas jawing away at the camera, perhaps they should be singing whilst they decorated their classroom with pretty Christmas streamers and shining silver baubles. Yes, that would be suitably excruciating; we could even add a little artificial snow to the corners of the windows and film it all on a star-filter so the lights would wink and sparkle at the camera.

As always, the reality was in sharp contrast to the conception.

167

The school choir appeared to be made up almost entirely of sadistic hooligans. Half were punk-like creatures, floating about in a daze, kicking anything that moved; half looked like a bunch of dishevelled 17th-century pugilists searching for a punch-up. Both sides united in a common objective: to make our life hell. They succeeded.

As I watched them tear apart the decorations and knock over desks and benches, I tried to work out how they had ever actually managed to record a song — perhaps they'd been bribed by free supplies of glue, or the offer of a few rabied dogs to kick to death. It certainly seemed to be beyond *us*. At one point Mike looked as though he was on the point of being mugged, despite the coachloads

*The school choir.*

of extra staff brought in to try to prevent his camera equipment from being stolen. Making myself heard above the shouts and screams of these small but highly effective organs of destruction was exhausting; getting them organised was harder still. Also, for the music sequence to work the song would have to be mimed on several separate takes, which made it worse. For the first, the camera would be in a fixed, wide-angled position for a master shot;

the song must then be repeated two or three times so that Mike could move in closer and shoot a selection of close-ups to add to that master.

After an hour and a half of chaos it became clear that, like the Titanic, we were heading on an unwavering disaster course. Don had already allocated a large slab of the programme to the song so to inform him at such a late stage that the film wouldn't make it would probably send him into paroxysms of despair.

It was with some relief, then, that I received a message from an embattled teacher, who had forced his way into the room, that I was required on the telephone. Leaving Mike and Tim barracaded into a corner behind a row of benches, like Custer's Last Stand, I beat a hasty retreat to the door, amidst much jeering and hurling of unpleasant missiles such as pieces of chalk and inky balls of paper.

It was Don.

'Nige, we think an IRA bomb has gone off in the middle of Tidworth on Salisbury Plain. Sorry to interrupt your nice little Christmas record film, but please get over there with Mike as fast as possible. National news want it as well, of course.'

This was the best news I'd heard all day.

IRA activity in our part of the world had been diminishing after a series of successful arrests and prosecutions. The cell that had planned the destruction of the QE2, for example, had been broken up and its members were beginning long prison sentences. Nevertheless, the IRA was still on people's minds. Only a few weeks before, Enid had walked pale and trembling into the office after the windscreen of her car had shattered. 'When I heard the crack of the glass I dived down onto the seat,' she had told me. 'I thought it was an IRA assassination attempt.' Why dear Enid considered herself to be the IRA's number one target I shall never know.

Perhaps this Tidworth incident signalled the start of a new campaign. Perhaps this was my big chance with television news.

Normally a film crew takes an eternity to pack up its gear and get moving; on this occasion, still under seige from the rioting choristers, Mike and Tim moved faster than I had ever seen them. We were out of that building and on our war to the military garrison town of Tidworth within seconds. On the way I talked excitedly to Don on the radio. Details were still coming in, but it now wasn't clear whether the bomb — apparently found in a newsagent's shop in the centre of town — had actually exploded. Nevertheless, London were desperate for pictures.

It was a narrow, winding road to Tidworth and every juggernaut, veteran car and learner-driver in central Southern England was using it at that moment. Precious time was slipping by. The slower the traffic, the more nervous I became. I thought the centre of town might well be cordoned off, creating more delays; there could be large crowds blocking access roads, as well as diversions, police road checks and fleets of ambulances standing by to take away the wounded. Making the early evening bulletins would be difficult.

The steering wheel became damp with the sweat from my fingers.

At last, we reached Tidworth and, with Mike following me in his lumbering old van, we cruised around looking for the centre of activity. Everything, however, appeared alarmingly normal. This was a small country community doing nothing more sinister than going quietly about its daily business. Small groups of children were hopping and skipping their way home from school. Mothers with prams and old ladies with small, sniffing dogs wandered peacefully in the park. A butcher was shutting up shop.

Eventually, I spotted the newsagent's shop that had been named as the target of the bomb attack. I studied it with growing unease; it looked precisely like any other newsagent's shop. A grubbly little boy was leaning nonchantly on the distinctly unshattered shop front sucking a giant gob-stopper, at his feet a scraggy mongrel cocking his leg against a news-stand which bore the headline: RATES QUERY — COUNCIL SEEKS ASSURANCE.

As Mike parked his van, I walked quickly over to the shop. Inside there was a long queue of people waiting to buy their evening paper. I marched straight up to the counter but a stocky, very muscular little man stopped me with his arm and demanded: ''Ere, what's your game, cock? There's a queue here!'

'I'm from . . .'

'Wait yer turn, cock, we're all in a hurry here.'

Rather foolishly, I joined the end of the queue, which inched its way forward so slowly that my spine began to tingle with frustration. I considered bursting to the front again but the wretched little man was now glaring at me from the other side of the shop, eyeing me as though I were a hazard to public safety. The queue moved forward with a sudden, short burst, and then went aground again with an old lady suffering from Parkinson's disease immediately in front of me who couldn't decide which sort of lozenge stood the best chance of curing her sort throat. Nodding dizzily from side to side, she mumbled over this one and that until I could stand it no longer.

'Look, I'm sorry to butt in, but I'm from ...'

'Do you mind?' interrupted the shopkeeper, very loudly. He was a tall, intimidating man and he glowered at me.

Gradually, slowly, maddeningly, the old lady drew towards a final decision. Then, after emptying her handbag on the counter to find some loose change, she at last had the chosen lozenges in her shaky hand and was beginning to shuffle her way out.

I leapt forward, the words gushing out of me in merciful release: 'I'm from BBC television. We heard you had a bomb in this shop this afternoon. Is that right?'

Everyone in the shop turned in mild astonishment to listen.

'Bomb? Bomb? What bomb?' demanded the shopkeeper. He looked vaguely insulted.

'I'm sorry, we were under the impression that a bomb had been discovered here this afternoon. Some mistake?'

Suddenly the man started to chuckle.

'Oh, *that* bomb — yes, yes, now I'm with you.'

Everyone started to chuckle.

'What bomb would that be?' I eventually asked, in the absence of any explanation.

'Oh, an off-duty soldier found a suspicious package which looked rather like one of the bombs that went off in London last week. We called the disposal team and they blew it up.'

The story was beginning to look decidedly wobbly. I looked around me in the hope of seeing at least a modest area of devastation which could provide us with a few pictures. A blackened wall, perhaps, or roof rafters hanging down from a gaping hole in the ceiling, shattered glass everywhere, that sort of thing.

'Did they blow it up here, in the shop?' I asked, faced with nothing more than neat, careful lines of newspapers, books, magazines and greetings cards, wall to wall.

'Oh yes, come and look,' said the shopkeeper, warming to the subject.

This was baffling. There seemed to be no damage anywhere; but, nevertheless, I followed the man across the shop to a corner where he suddenly dropped to his knees and, with his face very close to the carpet, he began searching the floor like someone who had lost a contact lense.

'What are you looking for?'

'Ssssshh!' said the man, deep in concentration. I was just beginning to consider the possiblity that he had gone off his head when he let out a sharp yelp and said: 'Yes, yes, there it is!'

I stared down to where he was pointing triumphantly. At first I couldn't see anything; then, as I drew nearer, I made out a tiny black piece of burnt carpet about half the size of a fingernail.

'What's that?'

'That's it! That't where they blew it up!'

I looked again, hard, at the little black splodge.

'Didn't exactly do much damage, did it?'

'Oh it doesn't these days, you know. The detonation charge these disposal chaps use is very small indeed. That's all it needs. Of course, if it had been a real bomb it would have brought down the entire shop.'

It just didn't seem fair. Had we arrived at the scene a little earlier and got a few shots of the area being cordoned off, as brave disposal men risked their lives to tackle what could be a bomb powerful enough to blow them to pieces, London would have been happy. Even a couple of shots of a broken window might just have saved my self-respect.

But that! A minute, pathetic piece of charred carpet, no bigger than a few drops of spilt coffee, which you wouldn't have crossed the road to look at?

I felt near to weeping again.

Mike even had to trot out to fetch his special close-up lens to ensure the black mark would register on film; he and Tim were giggling so much it was in severe danger of being wobbled out of shot anyway.

I did try to explain to London over the telephone but they insisted I send up my cut story. I'm afraid it must have looked rather comical. Don was forced to use it on our own programme to fill the gap left by the singing vandals but, of course, it never got near the network news.

Afterwards, the News Organiser telephoned. 'Why on earth didn't you tell us it was such a tiny little blob? It looked crazy, like an April Fool's joke.' He was laughing with disbelief.

'I did tell you.'

'Still, at least you were wearing a tie.'

Who wanted to work in London anyway? I was happy here with the sea on one side and the beautiful Hampshire countryside on the other, with my flattering fête invitations and boring chief constables and three-legged donkeys. Here I had friends, here I was known, recognised, respected. Who wanted to be submerged in the anonymity of the noisy, dirty metropolis, where programmes had huge staffs and huge budgets and celebrities grew on trees?

The next day I had a call from a London editor who was looking for presenters for a new network programme. Was I interested?

'You bet!' I said.

# 12

There was only one way to capitalise on the opportunity to be a reporter on a London-based programme and that was to work like a demon. Such invitations, once abused, were rarely repeated. I was placed on three months' probation, at the end of which I must return to Southampton, there either to work out my notice gleefully with the promise of a glittering permanent posting in London, or there to remain, probably for the rest of my career, and no doubt armed with several unsubtle suggestions that if I ever dared venture within a thirty-mile radius of the Metropolis I would be met by a barrage of bargepoles.

I worked long, long hours filming in freezing, uncomfortable locations in some of the most isolated areas of Britain and not one word of complaint passed my shivering lips. It was a bitter winter and I am a man who prefers the little comforts of life, viz. bedroom slippers waiting beside a blazing log fire, hot-water bottle in bed ready for early night, etc. but such was my enthusiasm to prove I could get the job that I forced myself to leap for joy whenever a particularly gruelling shoot was suggested. How about making a film about a tank regiment on overnight exercise in the exposed, snow-swept wastes of Salisbury Plain? 'Gosh, yes, whacko, cracking idea, what fun, when can we get started?' Farrell pipes up immediately and everyone's impressed. Then 24 hours of sheer torture as the chilled drops of rain that somehow manage to find a way through the thermal underwear begin to turn into frost against the skin. No fires are allowed, of course; might give our position away to the enemy, what? Jolly good point, who needs fires anyway? asks Farrall, rubbing his hands together with pleasurable anticipation, inwardly groaning with utter misery.

I got so cold standing around making a film about the Postman of the Year, who just happened to deliver his round to a series of hillside villages on the high ground to the west of Berwick on Tweed, pummelled night and day by piercing winds sweeping in from the North Sea, that on one or two occasions I actually heard myself wailing aloud like a sick dog. It was rather a distant, ghostly wail and it took me some moments to realise it was I who was making it. The discovery shook me, I can tell you. It was so cold that I found myself passing through two distinct phases, rather like seasickness: a) feeling I'm going to die, and b) wanting to die.

Nevertheless, back at base, amidst cries of 'Bet your balls were frozen off up there!' it was a case of 'Hardly noticed the temperature, actually, too busy lining up good shots,' etc., etc.

Everything about London was bigger, more complicated, more remote. I worked in an office which was part of an old film studio complex, built like a rabbit warren. Over the years more tunnels, passages and corridors were added so haphazardly that even those old codgers who had been there from the start spent half their time lost. Finding the way to and from my desk would take up a major part of the day; it was no use asking passers-by for help because of course they, too, would be lost.

The chap who had survived the famous pig-biting incident had suddenly become a tiny cog in a gargantuan wheel. Not that I minded the anonymity; in many ways it was most refreshing. What was difficult to accept was that I was no longer part of a small, intimate team where each contribution was vital to the success of the whole. Now, if my film wasn't ready by the deadline, there was no Don pacing up and down staving off delirium; it was simply dropped from the programme and another quickly found to fill its place.

Gone, too, was the intimacy of our scruffy old reporters' room. My new desk sat in a giant, open-plan office with an air-conditioning system so ruthlessly efficient that at the height of the hottest summer staff went to work equipped with thick jumpers and woolly scarves and in winter, with outside temperatures plummetting towards absolute zero, we padded about barefoot and in T-shirts. Worst still, here there was nowhere to hide from prowling producers and editors. Anyone suffering even mildly from agrophobia would have gone off the rails by coffee-break on day one.

Working on films for a national audience meant much bigger film crews, too. Reporters no longer directed their own films, they worked with directors and producers so that editorial decisions had to be shared, a source of great potential friction to someone like me, so used to working alone. The cameraman was now much more of an imperious figure, barking out orders to his assistant and to his electrician. There were so many film crews available that one rarely worked with the same group of people twice. Arriving on location we had to introduce ourselves to the crew as well as the interviewee; suddenly I found I missed Ron and Mike, even if they were always late or disappearing to rip up any grass nearby.

Filming budgets were larger, of course, and whilst this meant we could be more ambitious it also meant standards were higher, too. Films had to be good, they had to be *right*, or you were in trouble.

We shot a film about the pilot of a small biplane who intended to fly in his open-cockpit machine over the peak of Mount Everest to commemorate the very first such flight 50 years ago. We met him making final preparations for the trip on a small, grass airfield near the appropriately named Biggleswade.

The director was a formidable-looking man with straight black hair and a vast, black, handlebar moustache with ends like pieces of ornamental wrought-iron and which encroached over so much of the rest of his face that it made him look like a wild boar. The wrought-iron bits began to quiver whenever he grew excited — a disarming sight — but I did my best to ignore this phenomenon whilst we discussed how best to shoot the film. Eventually, we decided that I would stand at the end of the airfield and record a piece-to-camera so timed that as I was speaking the biplane would actually appear behind me and take-off over my head. You will understand that this involved perfect timing and an absence of any fluffs in my delivery — a fact the wild boar seemed to take some delight in constantly reminding me. I had only three sentences to say but his big build-up made me more nervous than usual and from deep within my entrails there was a growing suspicion that a cock-up lay just over the horizon.

This one piece-to-camera took most of the afternoon to set up. The exact camera position, for example, took half-an-hour to find. So did the precise starting-point for the beginning of the biplane's take-off. We were even equipped with walkie-talkies so that we could talk directly to the pilot but the sound of the plane's engine was so great in the cockpit that the poor fellow couldn't hear a word; this meant that if there was even a slight change to our immaculately planned procedure hacked out beforehand the wild boar had to lumber off down the runway, bellow the new instructions into the pilot's inner ear, then lumber all the way back. Since we were several hundred yards apart this took even more time and nearly killed the rather overweight wild boar.

All was set eventually and we were just about to cue the pilot when the heavens opened and we were subjected to a tropical monsoon. Our cars were half-a-mile in the other direction and we got so soaked that even the wrought-iron bits on the moustache began to droop depressingly.

Finally, the skies cleared, we set up again, the cameraman annouced he was ready for Take Two. We all jumped up and down to cue the pilot, and the little plane began to taxi slowly down towards us.

The take-off was perfect; the camerawork was immaculate; the sound recording was beyond criticism; I fluffed my lines.

The wild boar blew a fuse.

'. . . taking its own plate into history.'

It was only a little slip. Instead of saying: '. . . and soon this tiny plane will be taking its own place in history' I said: '. . . and soon this tiny plane will be taking its own *plate* into history' which I'll grant you is a little confusing. Where the word 'plate' popped up from I do not know. In regional television we would probably have said 'Oh sod it!' and forgotten the whole thing. Not now.

'Let's try again, shall we?' asked the wild boar, very softly. I noticed with alarm that the wrought-iron bits were twitching spasmodically with irritation. Then he drew a deep breath and heaved himself off down the runway, flapping his arms wildly as though competing in some medieval birdman rally. I wondered for a moment if the strain wasn't beginning to tell when I realised that he was trying to attract the attention of the biplane now circling patiently overhead. After an age that pilot seemed to get the message that a retake was required and he came in to land.

Now it's normal convention in this business that when the reporter has made a mistake, his director, being a gentleman, and wishing of course to avoid offending his artiste's sensibilities, politely apologises to all those involved and explains the shot must be done again because of a minor technical problem.

In this case, I'm afraid, the sensibilties of the artiste involved were not taken fully into account.

'We'll have to do it again, I'm afraid, because my bloody reporter made a cock-up, didn't he?' the wild boar shouted at the pilot, trying to make himself heard above the scream of the propeller.

The pilot looked blank and leant forward, pointing at his ear.

'My bloody reporter has made a cock-up!'

The pilot shook his head and frowned.

'*I said my bloody reporter made a cock-up!*'

At the time I thought all this was a bit thick, particularly because he was shouting so loudly that most of Biggleswade could have picked up the gist of the conversation, but I let it pass. On Take Three, after waiting for another monsoon to pass overhead and paying a large sum in cash for the pilot to fill up his aircraft with fuel, I managed to get it right, just as dusk descended.

We had spent so much time and money on that 30-second sequence that I was convinced I would be condemned to a life sentence in Southampton as soon as reports of the action filtered back to my new editor. But standards had changed. The editor loved the shot, brushed aside any worries about cost, and shortly afterwards offered me a one year London contract.

It took me between two and three seconds to make up my mind.

178

'I'll take it,' I said, feeling like a man who had stumbled into a pot of gold whilst out walking the dog in the park.

I had to return to Southampton to work out two months' notice before taking up my new post and as soon as I walked into the reporters' room I knew I had chosen the right moment to move on. Even though I had been away only a short time, there was a wind of change about. For example, the reporters' room had — wait for it — been redecorated. The walls had been painted a ghastly shade of green; the curtains were brand new and looked suspiciously as though they might actually meet up in the middle when drawn. The old pieces of typewriter and broken telephones and empty wine glasses which had made the place feel like home were nowhere to be seen.

Now that I was leaving they had even managed to find me a desk — my very own desk.

I felt like a stranger.

There was a sudden crash and the hatchway burst open. Out popped the familiar contours of Don's head. He noticed me standing there, a little lost, and he gave me a huge smile. His torso was stretching out into the room so enthusiastically that the cigarette he was holding was squashed against him and was burning a small brown hole in his huge off-white jumper.

'Hello, mate!'

'Hello, Don!'

I detected something was different. I had never seen Don looking so cheerful. Hysterical, yes; cheerful, no.

'Are you all right, Don!'

'Fine, mate!'

'Not ill?'

Don shook his head violently.

'I'm retiring.'

I began to notice a pungent smell of burning. I immediately remembered the cigarette. At any moment Don's beaming figure was about to be engulfed in flames. I pointed this out. Don casually beat out the smouldering jumper with the ease of an experienced fireman. Still smiling, the face withdrew through the smoke-screen and the hatch banged shut.

The next moment the door opened and there was Jenni. She, too, was grinning.

'Hello Nige!'

'Hello Jenni!'

Her eyes were sparkling like diamonds. I had never seen her looking so good.

'Guess what?' she said at length.

Now I don't know about you, but I've always found this question a stickler to answer. I mean, the range of possibilities is enormous. The chances of hitting the correct answer in one go must be pretty remote.

'What?'

'I'm engaged!'

Now this was a shock. Jenni engaged? It didn't seem possible.

'Engaged? Who to?'

'Dave!'

'Dave?'

'A submariner from Gosport! And we intend to have a family!'

This was harder still to swallow. Somehow Jenni and gurgling babies with doubtful nappies didn't quite seem to go hand in hand. Nevertheless she seemed pretty keen on the idea and, her mind no doubt brimming over with thoughts of love and adoration, dimples and burps, Jenni skipped off. I had never seen Jenni skip before. Most unsettling.

I thought I had better sit down and had just managed to reach a chair when the door opened a second time. It was Enid. She was apparently in conversation with someone several miles away.

' — and tell him not to do a thing until he's spoken to me first or else there'll be real trouble. And don't forget to warn him that Ron won't be there until twelve at least — Hello, Nigel! — and he's got to take some extra rolls of film with him, Newcastle want a version.'

'Hello, Enid!'

'Hello, Nigel. Nice to have you back. Don says would you mind popping up to Reading to interview a man who's taught his Tarantula to tapdance?'

I breathed a huge sigh of relief. At last normality had returned.

Those last few weeks in Southampton had a rather sad quality about them. Not only was there a mood of great change in the air; but I began to see that the very pressures I had been moaning about for the last three years whereby reporters were expected to find, direct and report their own film stories, present programmes in the studio, newsread and make plenty of contributions to other programmes on the network — in short a television jack-of-all-trades — was the very element I would miss most. It was only much later when I was in London that I realised what a superb training it had been — and what a great advantage it was to prove.

We organised a leaving party for Don and as the day drew near he grew less and less enthusiastic about the prospect of imminent retirement. 'I'm going to miss all you buggers hurling abuse at me all day,' he confided to me mournfully. 'And the evenings just won't be the same without a good post-mortem and bollocking from Himself.'

In a way Don's leaving party was my leaving party, too. El Vino flowed in handsome quantities, as you might expect, and after tearfully swearing eternal allegiance to everyone I ended the evening in distinguished fashion by actually falling down a sewer.

It happened in a dark alley just outside the hotel we had taken over for the night. Bruce, Jenni and I were propping each other up and waving goodbye to the departing guests when I suddenly found myself disappearing from view and plunging at high speed into the bowels of the earth.

For a moment I thought I had suddenly died and was passing through purgatory en route to hell, for I appeared to be descending into a black, echoing cave which was filled with the most appalling smell ever to assault my delicate nostrils. Then, gradually, I realised I had in fact stepped into a small manhole in the road which rather unfortunately lacked a cover. If it hadn't been for Bruce and Jenni hauling me out I should probably still be there to this day; and such was the effect of the hangover the following morning that it took the best part of quarter-of-an-hour to work out why my socks, shoes, trousers and shirt-tails were smelling as though they had just been dragged out from the depths of a Saharan cess-pit.

On my last day at Southampton, Don trapped me in a corner and said he had a final little job for me.

'I want you to go out in style,' he said, ominously.

'But Don, this is my last —'

'I've had a brilliant idea.'

The following week the wreck of Henry VIII's warship, the Mary

Rose, was due to be lifted from the sea bed of the Solent a mile off Portsmouth Harbour. The run-up to the lift had been given huge publicity and as part of the enormous coverage already planned for the raising itself, Southampton were preparing a special programme about the history of the ship. As a contribution to this Don had arranged for me to dress up in Tudor costume and be taken out in a small hired boat to the site of the wreck. There I was to film a report as though I were a Tudor Alan Whicker giving details of the sinking of the Mary Rose, which would then of course have been a major story.

It was a clever idea but, I could see, fraught with potential elephant traps. And it *was* my last day.

'Don, this may not be as easy as you imagine.'

'It'll be a piece of cake.'

'All right then, you come with me and direct it.'

As Don was also leaving at the end of that week, and since his replacement as producer of the programme had already arrived, I knew that for once he was free to leave the office for a few hours. There was no excuse.

'I haven't shot a film for years,' he said, flannelling desperately. Then suddenly his eyes seemed to light up with the old sparkle of someone who would never — quite — lose his appetite for the excitement of television. 'You're on!' he said at length. 'I've fixed up the boat to leave at 10.40 from the dockyard so if the crew is there quarter of an hour before we'll have time . . .'

That afternoon the weather turned bad. By the time we had set off out of Portsmouth Harbour in our little boat — with me, I might add, splendidly dressed in authentic Tudor costume, with cap and feather, doublet and hose hired from a local theatre — there was a fierce force eight gale blowing. As we passed through the harbour entrance and hit the first of the heavy rollers sweeping in from the Channel the boatmen asked if we wanted to turn back.

'Not likely,' Don said quickly. 'Can't afford to come back and do this again another day.'

We had to smash our way through the waves, against the power of the shrieking wind. Gradually, we clawed our way out towards the salvage vessel that lay anchored directly above the wreck. On board we could see some of the divers scurrying for shelter as vast

182

*The Tudor reporter.*

black storm clouds billowed up high above.

By the time we reached the Mary Rose marker buoy we were all — even Mike the cameraman, this time — feeling distinctly delicate. I said to Don: 'Let's get this in the can and run for it, for God's Sake,' and from its cowering position in the comparative shelter of the deckhouse a pale face nodded its agreement.

Mike started rolling and, grasping a stick microphone in my hand à la Whicker, I began my fatuous report. 'First details of the disaster indicate that the Mary Rose, which sank just a few yards from where I'm standing now, went down with all hands, and it's feared the death toll may be high.'

Just then I heard a voice wailing in the wind. It said: 'What the f... are you silly buggers doing?'

I stopped and, looking around, I saw a group of divers on the salvage ship a few hundred yards away who had braved the weather and were watching us. One or two of them were pointing at me and calling up others to come and look.

'We're filming!' I screamed back at them. 'For television.'

Just then, a huge wave crashed into the boat and the decking shuddered with the strain. For a few moments I was totally under water. Then, gasping for air, I managed to pull myself up.

Don was sprawled across the deckhouse floor, his cigarette at last extinguished. Mike was clinging on his camera with one hand and the wheel with the other. Tim the soundman was being sick over the side.

A voice from the salvage vessel was thrown across to us in the wind.

'You buggers must be f . . . crazy!'

I looked up at the ship which was now lined by rows of cheering divers. Then I looked down at my porous Tudor hosepipe tights, still bulging with seawater and sprouting little jets of liquid like a punctured bladder. Across my face I could feel the long, soaking feather from my Tudor hat which had stuck to my skin like a sodden flannel. A few yards ahead I could see another mammoth wave forming.

I looked at Don, and Don looked at me, and we both started to laugh.

Suddenly, the face of my old Polish professor at medical school appeared before me. As I braced myself for the thud of the next icy wave, I began to wonder if he'd consider having me back.